CW01645157

A Walk around the SNICKELWAYS OF YORK

by Mark W. Jones

SEVENTH EDITION

FIRST EDITION

Published	*June 1983*
2nd Impression	*July 1983*
3rd Impression	*October 1983*
4th Impression	*January 1984*

SECOND EDITION

Published	*April 1984*
2nd Impression	*July 1984*
3rd Impression	*April 1985*

THIRD EDITION

Published	*March 1986*
2nd Impression	*September 1987*

FOURTH EDITION

Published	*March 1989*
2nd Impression	*May 1989*
3rd Impression	*May 1990*

FIFTH EDITION

Published	*November 1991*

SIXTH EDITION

Published	*March 1993*
2nd Impression	*August 1994*

SEVENTH EDITION

Published	*January 1997*
2nd Impression (updated)	*October 1999*

Printed by Maxiprint
Kettlestring Lane, Clifton Moor, York YO30 4XF, England
www.maxiprint.co.uk

Published by

Mark and Ann Jones
April Cottage
Bulmer
York YO6 7BW
England

© 1997 Mark & Ann Jones

ISBN 0 9511158 4 7

FOREWORD

By John Shannon, C.B.E., D.Univ (York)

Chairman, York Civic Trust

A few years ago it was difficult to find books on York, but with the growth of tourism this has altered to such an extent that one would think that nothing new could be written about the City. But Mark Jones has discovered that there lies beneath and behind the great set pieces – The Minster, the Walls, the Guildhalls and Parish Churches – a wealth of charm and character, there to be explored and savoured at leisure. Indeed this is a book every bit as much for York citizens as for the tourist. York in the middle ages was a busy and thriving community with some ten thousand people living within its walls. They were not content simply to follow medieval street patterns which had been superimposed upon the Roman roads, but created for themselves what might be described as a human rabbit warren of alleyways, snickets, ginnels – 'The Snickelways of York' to use Mr. Jones' apt description. This book is essential reading for all who love their York and think they know it, and the excellence of the text is matched by the illustrations.

May 1983

ACKNOWLEDGEMENTS

I had no right at all to stumble, as an amateur, into the already expertly written-about, and copiously illustrated, history of our ancient city of York. That I have done so was not just because the Snickelways led me there: it was due to the help, encouragement, advice and criticism of many friends, colleagues and experts. In particular I should like to thank the ever-helpful and patient staff of the York Central Reference Library; the City Planning Department; and the City Archivist. They all sought out and found for me information on a range of unusual subjects, from public hangings to public conveniences, and from ancient title-deeds to building developments yet to come.

I also wish to express grateful thanks to John Shannon, who through his writings and public talks has stimulated in me – and I am certain in countless other York citizens – a fascination for the pleasures that await discovery with almost every step one takes through our city's by-ways.

As for the style of presentation of this book: All who have been guided up, down and around the Lakeland mountains by Alfred Wainwright's inimitable works will, I hope, recognise that this humble effort of mine was inspired by his technique. I have long been a devout admirer of his vastly informative combination of maps, drawings and commentary (which, because handwritten, can absorb personal and sometimes outrageous idiosyncracies!)

Finally I must thank my family, who have cheerfully endured even less undivided attention than usual from me – except, that is, when I have required attention from them. And that, as they are my sternest critics, has been quite frequently!

Mark Jones
May, 1983

INTRODUCTION

Ask anyone what York is famous for, and they'll talk about the Minster, the Walls, Museums, Railways, Races, Kit Kat... In fact, they'll say anything but Snickelways.

Yet York has a profusion of Snickelways. They thread their way from Minster to market, from Stonegate to Shambles, and from Whip-ma-whop-ma-gate to the Walls. Their names conjure up echoing footsteps on hollowed paving-stones, comings-and-goings in sunshine and shadow: *Pope's Head Alley, Coffee Yard, Lund's Court, Hornpot Lane, Black Horse Passage*...

Straker's Passage MWJ

Nearly all of them are historic, though most were never designed to be. They were, as often as not, simply the paths that people took – to work, to market, to church, and sometimes on less virtuous pursuits. They lend their own perspective to the history of the city.

So this book doesn't attempt to match the wealth of excellent works that you can read elsewhere about historic York, its buildings and landmarks. It deals instead – in a totally unscholarly, selective and personal approach – with these much humbler places called Snickelways. History is simply left to emerge piecemeal from their well-trodden past: a past embracing diverse centuries and lifestyles, majesty and misery, inspiration and squalor.

Some of our Snickelways are famous the world over. Others are so obscure that few – not even citizens of York – know of their existence.

This book, therefore, isn't only intended for the guidance of visitors: it's for anyone who enjoys discovery and surprise.

For the Snickelways of York abound in both.

M.W.J. May 1983

Bedern

MWJ 1984

Since this scene was sketched, the building on the left - formerly the Chapel of the Vicars Choral in the 14th century - has been restored, but in the form of a storage-room for the Minster.

INTRODUCTION TO THE SECOND EDITION

"Sitting in a sunlit room in the Home Counties, this citizen of York (albeit thirty years resident down here) is wandering in imagination through the Snickelways, lit by the same sun and with the great bell of the Minster striking twelve – or, as in the ever-lasting summer days of childhood, the smaller bells ringing out about tea-time ....."

This lovely passage of nostalgic writing, from a reader in St. Albans, perhaps helps to explain why "Snickelways" (as the book is called for short in York) seems to have attracted more people than we had any right to expect. Somewhere in all of us, apparently, lies a mixture of curiosity and nostalgia for these hidden and mostly inconsequential places.

So the book has found its way to places as diverse as Wigan and Washington, Harrogate and Hong Kong, Feltham and Finland, Manchester and Melbourne, Thorngumbald and Upper Volta.

Perhaps for this very reason, the Snickelways have not (as we might have feared) become thronged with ten thousand readers, struggling eternally and vainly to enter or escape these narrow fastnesses. Whether through choice or necessity, the majority of readers seem content to explore the Snickelways in the mind's eye. So the Snickelways have changed but little. They remain intimate, inviting, mostly quiet, and used only by people who are there because they want to be there.

But York does change; and this new edition is necessary to take account of some of the changes (including a brand-new Snickelway that has appeared!). It also enables me to make various alterations and additions, mainly arising from comments and suggestions from readers (including one encounter at the York Refuse Tip) for which I am most grateful.

Above all, people seem to be finding (as I do) that the Snickelways are fun. I hope that this will be your experience, too – whether you explore them in person, or whether, in company with our reader in St. Albans, you wander through them in your imagination.

M.W.J. February 1984

The River Foss and Rowntree Wharf
(See pages 54, 55 & 91)

MWJ 1985

INTRODUCTION TO THE FIFTH EDITION

When "Snickelways" was first published some eight years ago, it was neither intended nor expected to run to a second printing, never mind a fifth edition. But this has become necessary, for the single and happy reason that important changes have been taking place in York, and all for the better.

First and foremost, the whole of the heart of the city, during the main part of the day, has now become a fit place for people on foot. Eight years ago, York had only two footstreets. Now, footstreets abound. Indeed, it might be argued that the main raison d'être of the walk around the Snickelways – to get away from the traffic – has now been removed, and for the best of reasons. Shall we say that the footstreets and the Snickelways complement each other. The Snickelways are themselves footstreets, only more so, as they remain uninvaded by traffic throughout the day and night.

Secondly, complementary to but quite distinct from the above, we have the closure of DEANGATE. It is now closed to traffic for good, in every sense of the word. Peace has already been restored to the Minster; and during the years to come we can look forward also to the restoration of dignity and beauty to its southern setting.

Thirdly, York has at last awakened to the significance and promise of its second river, the Foss. Thanks to the initiatives of the Yorkshire Evening Press and the Rowntree Foundation, the river within the city is becoming alive again. In celebration, I have added another "optional extra" walk, using the footways generously provided and improved by the Rowntree Foundation.

Finally, the City Council has commendably come to grips with the litter problem. We should blame British behaviour, not the City Council, for the fact that we still don't compare with the litter-free excellence of many cities on the Continent. But there has been a vast improvement.

These changes for the good all show what can be achieved when enlightened thinking is allowed to prevail, in both the public and the private domain. The benefits are ours to enjoy as we continue happily on our walk around the Snickelways.

Mark Jones

1991

CONTENTS

ILLUSTRATIONS

ABOUT the MAPS

1. General Map

Scale 1" = 110 yds

Fold-out, inside back cover

Identifies all the Snickelways by number and name, and shows the route of the Snickelways Walk as follows, in RED:

- Pedestrian access only
- Street with restricted, or very little, traffic.
- Street with normal traffic

The above symbols are used on other maps, but in BLACK.

2. Section Maps

Scale 1" = 110 yds

These show the subsections into which the walk is divided, and the relationship of the detail maps to each other map in the section. Each Section Map precedes its own Section.

Some Metric Conversions:

1" = 2.5 cm.	250 yds = 230 M	¼ = .25
110 yds = 100 M.	¼ mile = 402 M	1 pint
105 ft = 32 M.	1 mile = 1.6 KM	= .568 litres

3. Detail Maps

Mostly Scale 1" = 100 ft (app).

These show in detail each stretch of about 250 yards of the route. They usually accompany the relevant commentary on the same double-page.

Note that they are drawn so that you are usually walking up the page. (This means that NORTH has to shift around between one page and another. Each map shows where North has gone to, for the anxious few who worry about such things.)

Symbols on detail maps:

Public Conveniences: Ladies' / Gents' / Disabled

(P) : Public Car Park

PH : Public House

: Tree(s)

: Posts

Limit of commentary on preceding map

(14) (for example) Location of Snickelway

1¾ Miles from start at Bootham Bar (at ¼ mile intervals)

Recommended diversion for wheelchairists (See p. 88)

A SNICKELWAY IS....

There is no existing definition in the dictionary for a Snickelway. The nearest words (Collins English Dictionary) are:

"SNICKET (snikit):
Northern Brit. dialect: a passageway between walls or fences"

"GINNEL (ginl):
Northern English dialect: a narrow passageway between buildings"

"ALLEYWAY (aeliwei):
A narrow passage; alley"

Somewhere among these snikits, ginls and aeliweis lurks what we are looking for. So for convenience we take a bit of each:

(SNICK)ET GINN(EL) ALLEY(WAY)

Hence:

"SNICKELWAY (sniklwei):
A narrow passageway or alley between walls, fences or buildings"

But that isn't quite all. There are four other important characteristics of a Snickelway:

1. The public must have access to it (at least during daylight).
2. It must be solely or mainly used by people on foot.
3. It may also (in addition to the foregoing definitions) be a medieval lane, a public footpath or the top of a wall.
4. It must be a way through from one place to another.

So to sum it all up for the purposes of this book:

> A Snickelway is a narrow place to walk along, leading from somewhere to somewhere else, usually in a town or city, especially in the city of York.

To complete the definition, a Snickelway Family tree is shown opposite.

P.S.: A DISCLAIMER

A friend, who should know, now tells me that a SNICKLE is a SNARE in rural N. Yorks. Let's be clear: Poaching in the Snickelways is neither intended nor encouraged, nor likely to be very successful.

The Snickelway Species

SNICKELWAYS

- Paths
  - Enclosed
    - Between Walls
      - With Housefronts
        - Narrow — Alleys & Alleyways
        - Wider — Courts, Yards & Courtyards
      - Without Housefronts
        - Roofed — Passages & Passageways
        - Unroofed & Paved — Ginnels
    - Between fences, railings or hedges — Snickets
    - Between Shopwindows — Arcades
  - Open
    - Riverside — Walks & Staiths
    - Landbound — Precincts & Pathways
- Streets
  - Medieval — Common Lanes; Medieval Streets
  - Other — Footstreets
- Other Ways
  - Medieval Wall-tops — City Walls
  - Paths of Virtue — Churchyards

(Ginnels, Snickets:)
(a) A Snicket may also be between walls provided that it's unsurfaced
(b) Footsteps (except soft-shoes) ECHO in a GINNEL but not in a Snicket.

(Common Lanes, Medieval Streets, Footstreets:)
A line of posts may convert a Street into a Snickelway. (Even the Castle car park scrapes in by this means.)

THE WHEREABOUTS OF THE SNICKELWAYS

Having defined what a Snickelway is, we can now set about plotting where the Snickelways are.

It's a great temptation to start the list with the City Walls, for they are the longest and most splendid Snickelway of all. But there are already a host of excellent accounts of the Walls, so we won't presume to add to them; and in any case, most people have their own plans for seeing and walking round them. We therefore exclude them from our plotting.

There are also half-a-dozen Snickelways on the south-west side of the river, but they are rather isolated from the main cluster and from each other. So we'll omit them from the plot, along with one or two other outliers – though they are later summarised in the section on "optional extras" (Appendix 1).

This leaves us with the Snickelways Proper: those within the Walls, on the Minster side of the river. If we draw a box ½ mile long and ¼ mile wide, with Bootham Bar at one end and Clifford's Tower at the other, we collect a "bag" of no less than 50 Snickelways!

And because The Shambles is in the centre of the constellation, it follows that they must all lie within a quarter-of-a-mile of that most widely-known of York's narrowest streets. (But many are much narrower, both in dimension and repute...)

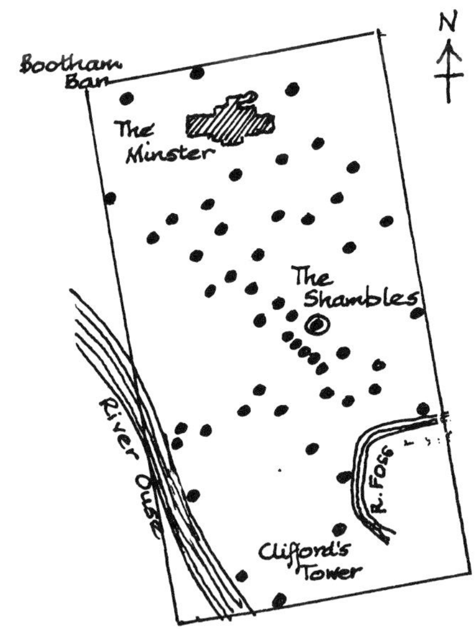

A. The Fifty Snickelways

THE SNICKELWAYS WALK

With such a profusion of them, the question was how to handle an account of the Snickelways. By district? Or in historical order? Or by category? Any of these approaches presented the danger of a somewhat hum-drum catalogue.

The answer was suggested by their very nature: They were all ways to walk along, so why not thread them all together into one continuous walk? This offered all sorts of bewildering possibilities: clearly some rules were necessary. So I have applied three simple ones:

1. Never to re-cross our path.
2. Never to retrace our steps.
3. To use traffic-ridden streets as little as possible.

There was one further consideration: some Snickelways demand that they are approached from a certain direction, to make the most of visual or atmospheric effect. I have tried to do this where it matters.

As diagram "B" shows, these rules lead to some very tortuous twists and turns. You easily become disorientated. The same landmarks keep cropping up unexpectedly, now from this angle, now from that.

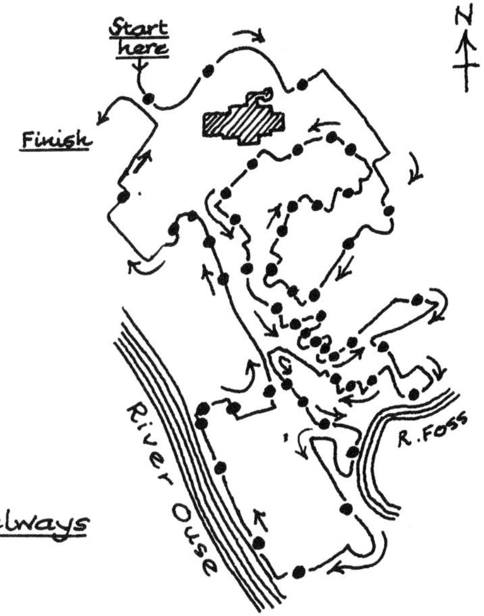

B. The Snickelways Maze

Occasionally you have to be careful to keep to the opposite side of a street which you traversed five minutes (or was it half-an-hour?) ago.

But if you follow the detail maps and stick to our rules, you'll find that it all works out in the end, as you finish through the southern arch of Bootham Bar. In fact, if you like you can then go right round the walls anti-clockwise, and still not re-cross your path until the final moment, at Bootham Bar.

TACKLING THE SNICKELWAYS

How you tackle the Snickelways will depend of course on your time, energy and the number of friends with whom you intend to start (and hope to finish - but more of that later).

The complete Walk of the Snickelways is 3½ miles long. But as you are never far from where you started, you can break it up into as many bits and pieces as you like. There are however some natural "short circuits", by which you can get back to Bootham Bar (the starting point) early, by switching from the main route, as follows:

SHORT CIRCUITS: Leave main route at:	Total coverage of circuit: Miles	Snickelways
a. St. Sampson's Sq. (1st visit)	1	12
b. " " " (2nd visit)	1½	24
c. Parliament Street	2½	38

From all the above, go straight into HORNPOT LANE NETHER (Map 23)

These are explained on the detail maps.

On the other hand, to make sure you don't lose the thread, you may feel like doing the lot in one go. 3½ miles within ¼ mile of The Shambles is quite an experience! Finally, if you still have the energy you can link up directly with the walk around the walls ("the 51st Snickelway") making it 6½ miles altogether.

Two final points:

First: Allow plenty of time, and take as long as you want. It will take you twice as long as you expect. The distractions will be legion. Quite apart from my own subjective, selective and disjointed narrative, and the complicated contortions of the route, you'll encounter everything from window-shoppers to men on ladders, and from rhubarb-sellers to Morris dancers. One Snickelway-mile is worth two of anything else in terms of time, interest and diversion.

Second: Whatever you do, walk the Snickelways in whichever way best suits you. The walk is there for enjoyment, not as an exercise in dutiful drudgery.

SAFETY IN NUMBERS?

You can of course explore the Snickelways on your own, and concentrate on their pleasures without distraction. But most of them are narrow, many dark, and some rather isolated. Personally I have always found the behaviour of fellow Snickelway-users impeccable. But you may not wish to go-it-alone, and far be it from me to discourage such prudence.

But at the other end of the scale, Snickelways don't lend themselves to large groups of people attempting to travel in crocodiles or other formations.

In the first place (unless every member of the party is armed with a copy of this guide) those at the back will become isolated and lost, never to be found again for the rest of the day, if ever.

Secondly, even if you don't lose people you'll lose time, in quite unbelievable quantities. The sudden onset of a group of (say) twenty people at a narrow Snickelway entrance can and will cause an almighty hold-up, to themselves and others.

Think of this: 50 Snickelways; 50 hold-ups at only two minutes a time... and this large party will spend _1¾ hours in a state of total inertia_, even with none but themselves to cope with. But throw in a few strangers inconsiderately intent upon progressing in the opposite direction (and there will in fact be many) and the loss of time reaches stupefying proportions.

Better, far, to keep your numbers small. Your progress will then be steady, sociable and serene.

AND SO TO THE START...

Coffee Yard (Map 11)

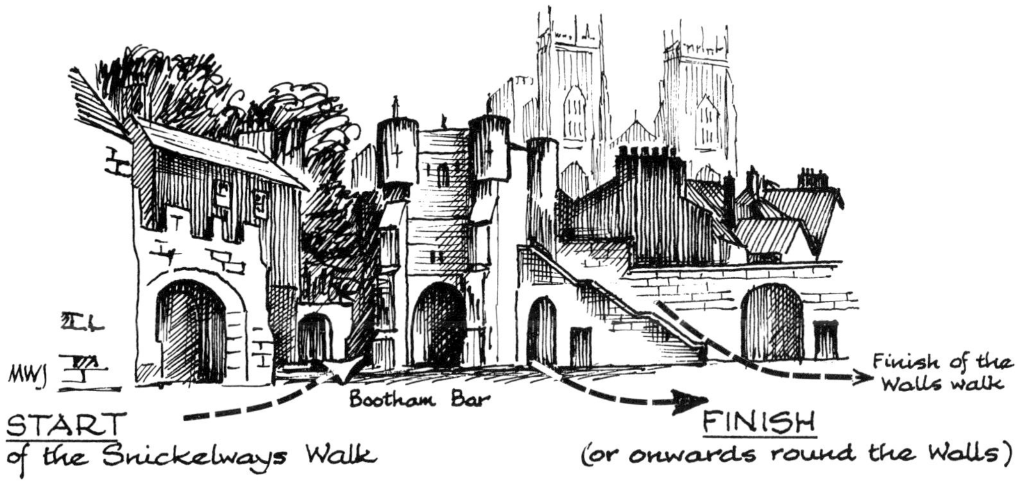

WHY START HERE?

There are three good reasons for starting from Bootham Bar:

In the first place, it's the most ancient of the old entrances into York. The others (Monk, Walmgate and Micklegate Bars) are a mere 700 years old. But there has been a gateway here for nearly 2000 years.

Secondly, Bootham Bar provides an ideal staging-post between our Snickelways walk and the walk round the Walls. Both begin and end here.

Thirdly, hardly have you started than you come to the first, shortest and perhaps the most delectable of all the Snickelways:

The perfect appetiser for what is to follow....

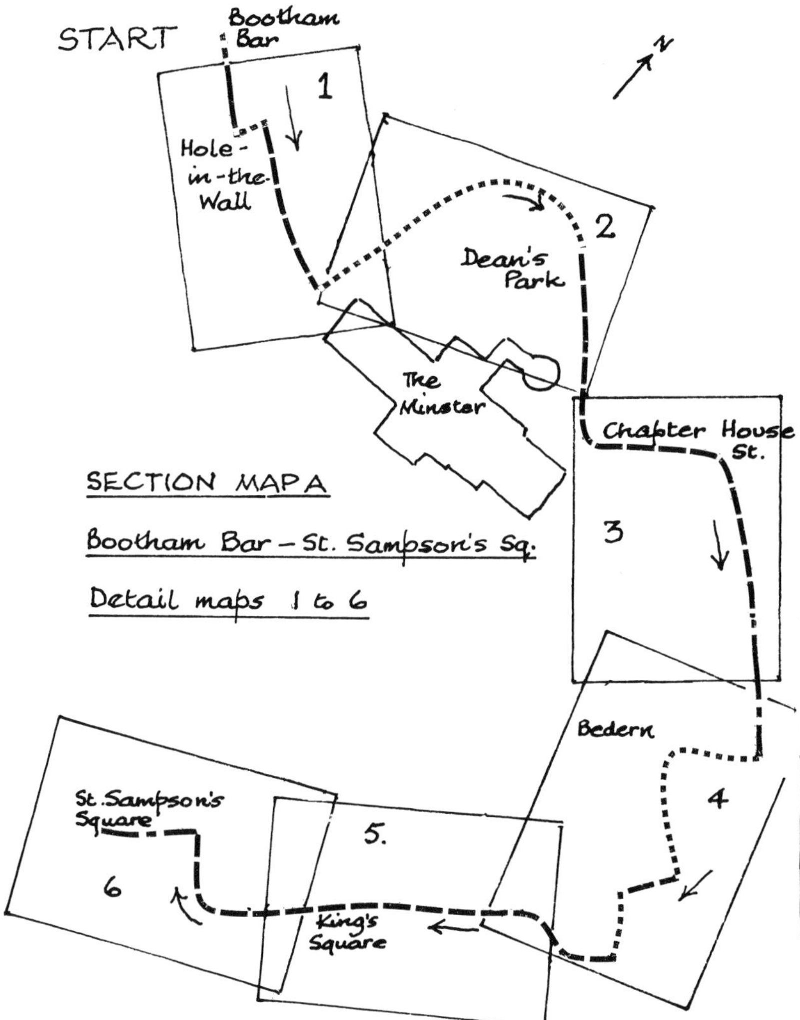

SECTION MAP A

Bootham Bar – St. Sampson's Sq.

Detail maps 1 to 6

Precentor's Court (through Hole-in-the-Wall)

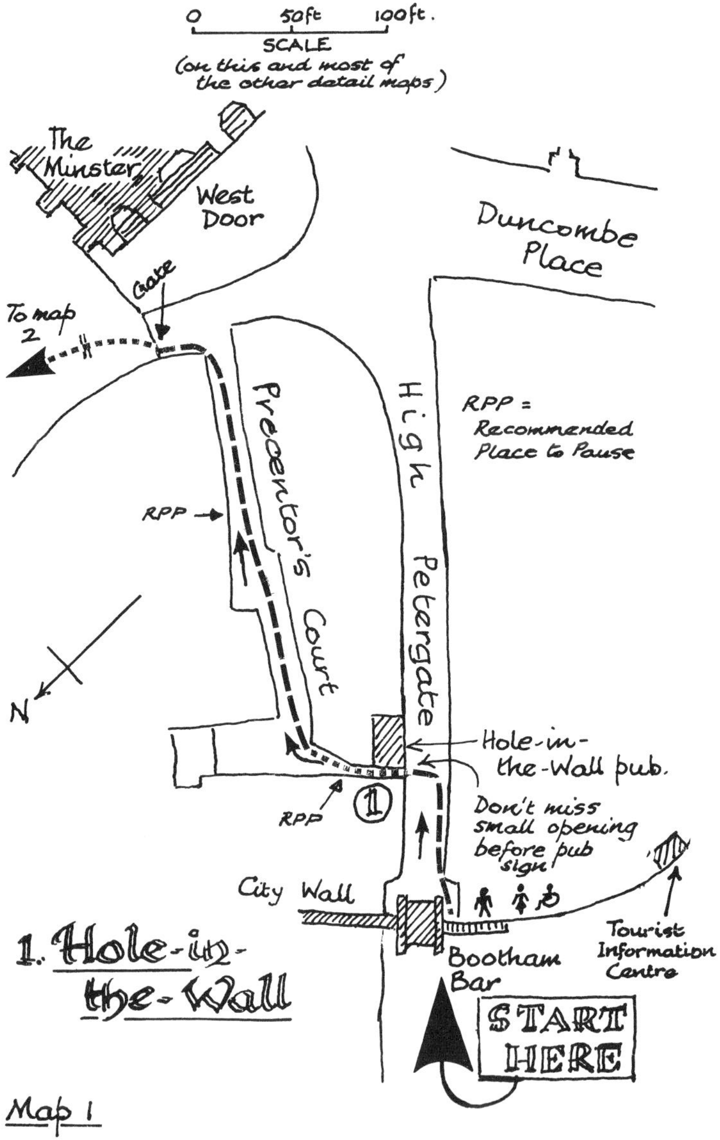

MAP 1 (Hole-in-the-Wall, Precentor's Court)

Our odyssey starts through the left-hand (pedestrian) archway of Bootham Bar into High Petergate, formerly the main cross-street (*Via Principalis*) of Roman York.

Very soon we come to the overhead sign of the Hole-in-the Wall pub – a recently-renovated hostelry whose name no doubt derives from the hole through which we've just entered the city. But our interest lies in another hole – the one hiding in the wall on the left, just before the sign.

This covered passageway suddenly wraps us in a mantle of tranquillity. Look back, and you can still see the hubbub of traffic and people, briefly framed in the archway as they hustle by in their different world. Look ahead, and you are in a peaceful courtyard, with elegant old houses, period street-lamps and quietness, probably without a soul in sight.

Move further out of this first Snickelway, and unexpectedly Precentor's Court, dating back to 1610, opens up on the right, to give you the most awe-inspiring of all the lovely views of York Minster. Above the narrow street and its graceful houses, the West Front soars majestically, its gleaming pinnacles two hundred feet above you.

No other street brings you so close to the sheer loftiness of those Minster towers. We can only wonder yet again at the inspiration, dedication, craftsmanship and downright human physical effort that went into the making of this immense and beautiful building, more than 500 years ago.

To find out more about Medieval building methods, it is well worth visiting (on a later occasion) The York Story (formerly the Heritage Centre, and originally St. Mary's Church) in Castlegate. This fascinating exhibition brings to life the day-to-day work and interests of the people of York in former times - the very times that are spanned by our Snickelways. *(See p.67)*

Precentor's Court and The Minster MWJ

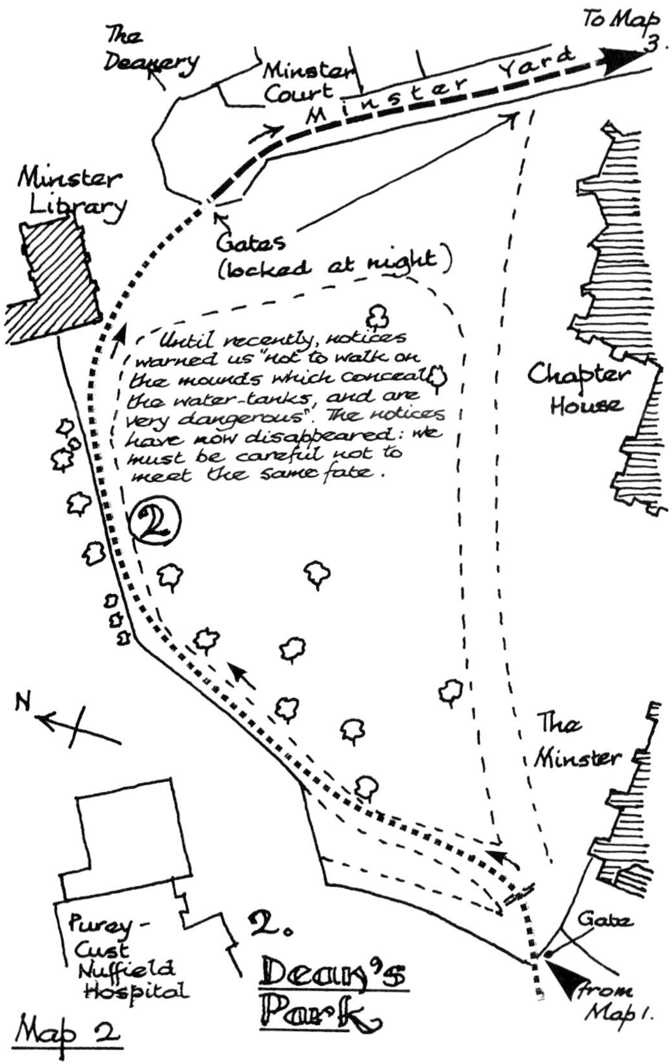

MAP 2 (Dean's Park)

Emerging from Precentor's Court, turn left through the gate into Dean's Park. Though no snicket or ginnel, this pleasant pathway has most of the attributes of a Snickelway: It's only for people on foot; it leads somewhere (towards the Minster Library and beyond); and best of all it takes us well beyond sight and sound of any vehicle (apart perhaps from the occasional delivery van on its way to Minster Court or The Deanery.)

Originally the site of the Roman Legionary fortress of Eboracum, which teemed with 6,000 men, Dean's Park now slumbers quietly around the Minster Library – almost all that is left of the 13th century Archbishop's Palace. It was here that, in 1483, Richard III invested his son as Prince of Wales. 330 years later, the building (which had been a chapel) became the Library.

As you stroll along the tree-lined path that curves off left towards the library, savour the peace, calm and dignity of this lovely part of the cathedral close. We'll need to draw upon this recollection later in our travels...

Dean's Park and the Minster Library MWJ

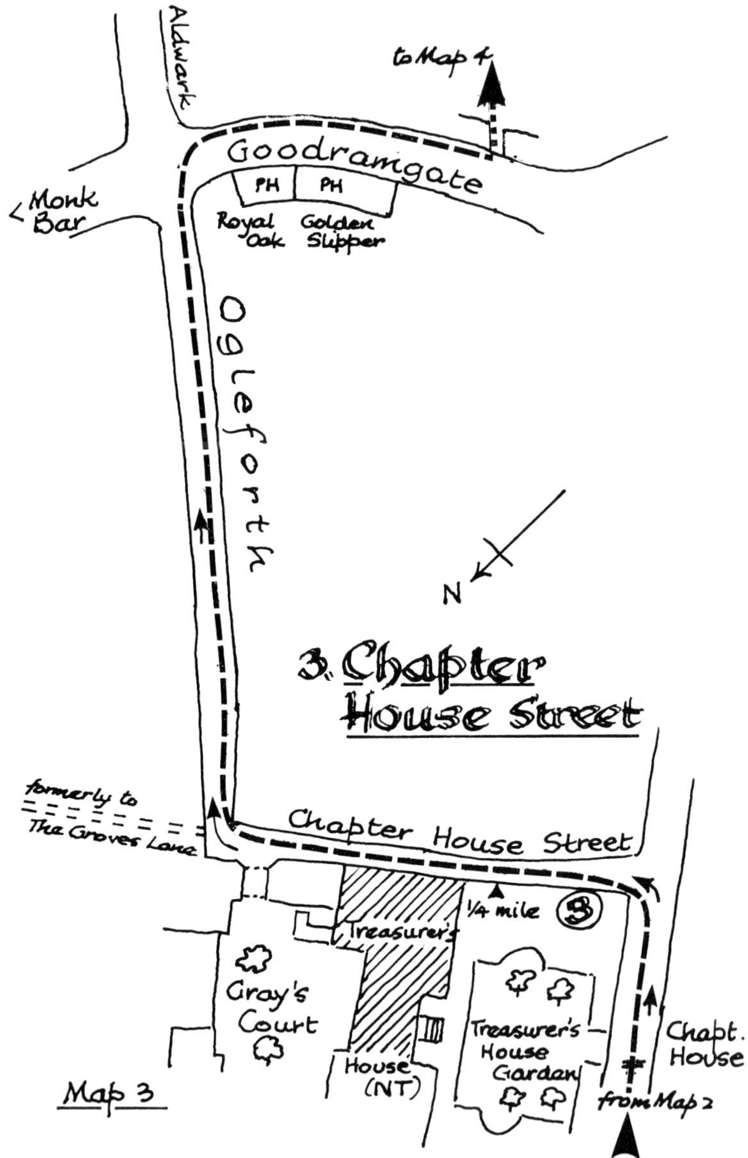

Map 3

MAP 3 (Chapter House Street & Ogleforth)

Leaving Dean's Park through the gateway, we turn right along the cobbled Minster Yard, past the tree-shaded Minster Court. Next is the Treasurer's House (1600). Strictly speaking this title relates to the site rather than the house, as the office had been dissolved by the time the building was completed. But this National Trust property demands a visit after you've completed the Snickelways – and what better place than its garden in which to rest, amid the sound of birdsong, bells and (perhaps) madrigals on a summer's afternoon?

We next turn left into Chapter House Street. Now quiet and secluded, this street was once the main Roman route (*Via Decumana*) to the north-east. Instead of turning its present corner into Ogleforth, it went straight on through a gateway in the fortress wall, and plunged out into the Forest of Galtres along the line of the surviving Groves Lane (an outer Snickelway: see page 84).

Just before the corner, on the left through the archway, is the attractive courtyard of Gray's Court – originally part of the Treasurer's House, and now used by the College of Ripon & York St. John. Round the bend we come into Ogleforth, formerly UGEL'S FORD. Though the latter sounds like a gurgling stream, it was probably (in 1100) an open drain, or worse.

The drain was probably "forded" at the same point by an earlier diagonal street which linked Goodramgate direct with the former Roman gateway, thus:

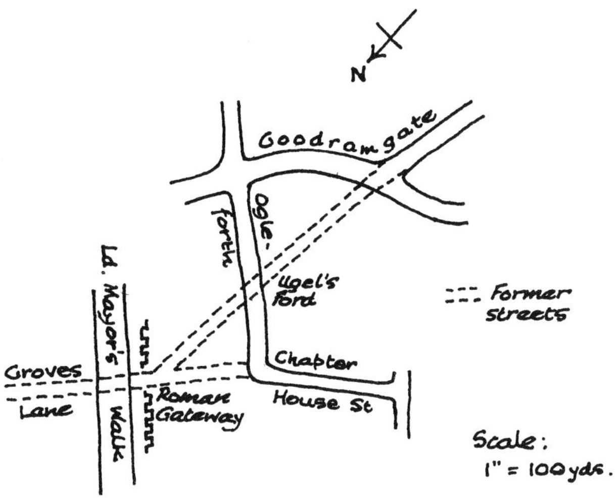

With the closure of Deangate (p. 41) and other traffic restrictions, it is now fairly safe for us to cross to the far side of Goodramgate, and follow it to the right for fifty yards or so (unless, that is, we wish to visit either of the adjacent hostelries on this side first.)

Ogleforth corner & Gray's Court MWJ

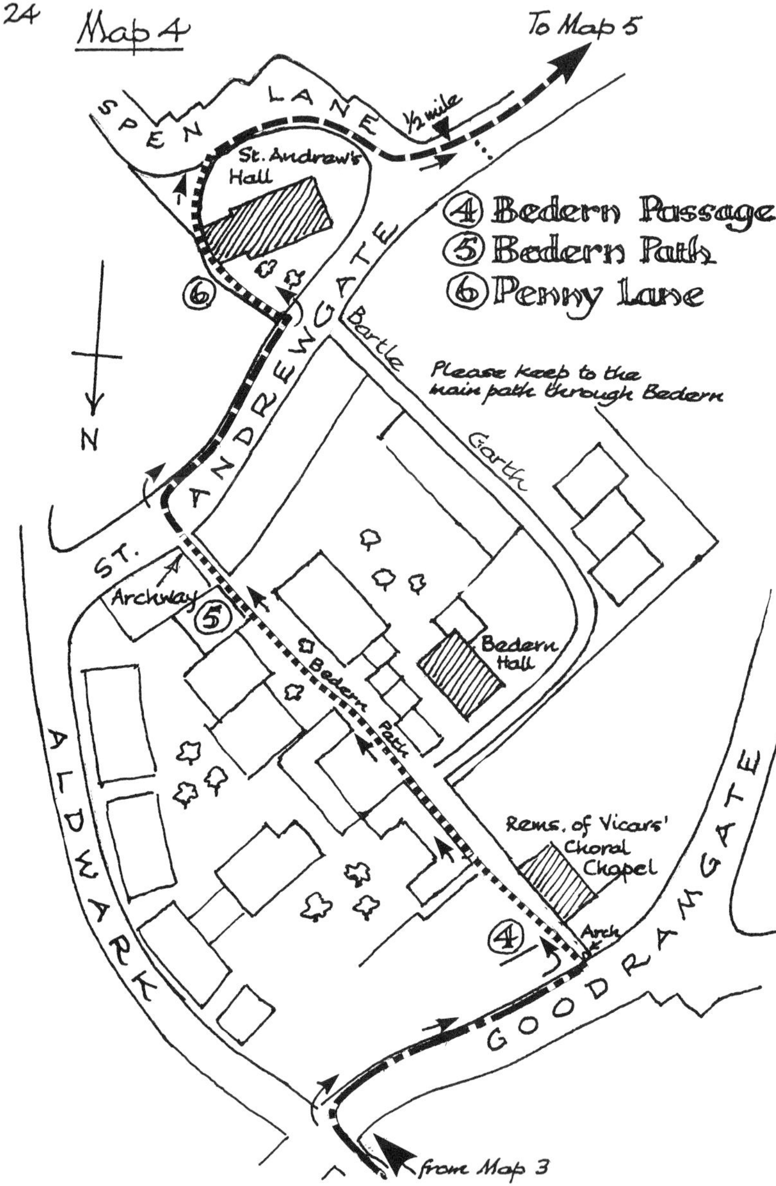

MAP 4 (Bedern)

"We present this project not solely as a solution to a specific problem in a unique historic city, but in the hope that it may be an example of the renewal and reoccupation of abandoned backland living-quarters of many old towns of Europe"

—So wrote Lord Esher in 1968; and now his far-sighted project has become a reality. People are actually living in Bedern again. In the 1970s only 3,500 of York's population lived within the city walls, compared with 10,000 in the Middle Ages. Now the tide has turned.

The Bedern has a chequered history. Originally adjoining the Minster precinct, it comprised the chapel, the hall and houses of the Minster's Vicars-Choral. But by the 1840s, this became an area of appalling slums, mostly lived-in by Irish immigrants – two-thirds of whom had only one room for the whole family. The poverty and disease led eventually to the clearance of the area – only for it to decline again, this time into a nondescript collection of workshops and warehouses. But now it will live again; and the new Bedern footpath (roughly along the line of the original medieval street) personifies this imaginative change for the good.

On our right are the remnants of the chapel of the Vicars-Choral (of which, I understand, a proposal is in hand for improvement and landscaping, in place of the present wilderness.)

Beyond, and further to the right, is the newly-restored Bedern Hall. It has a chequered past. Originally, in the 14th century, it was the dining-hall for the Vicars' Choral. But subsequently it was turned into tenements, became a mineral-water factory, and later was absorbed into a pork-pie works! But now it has been rescued and splendidly restored by the City Council and the Gilds.

Having turned right into St. Andrewgate, we quickly turn left again down Penny Lane, a short Snickelway skirting St. Andrew's Hall: originally part of a church, then a school, now a gospel-hall, and at some time in between a House of Ill Repute.

Our forebears used to take their handcarts through here: note the hub-height indentations! But now, alas, Penny Lane is obstructed by fearsome bollards and a trip-rail. We emerge into the former Ispingail, or "the lane overgrown with Aspens" (in 1161, that was).

Penny Lane

The buildings on the right have now disappeared, and new housing has taken their place.

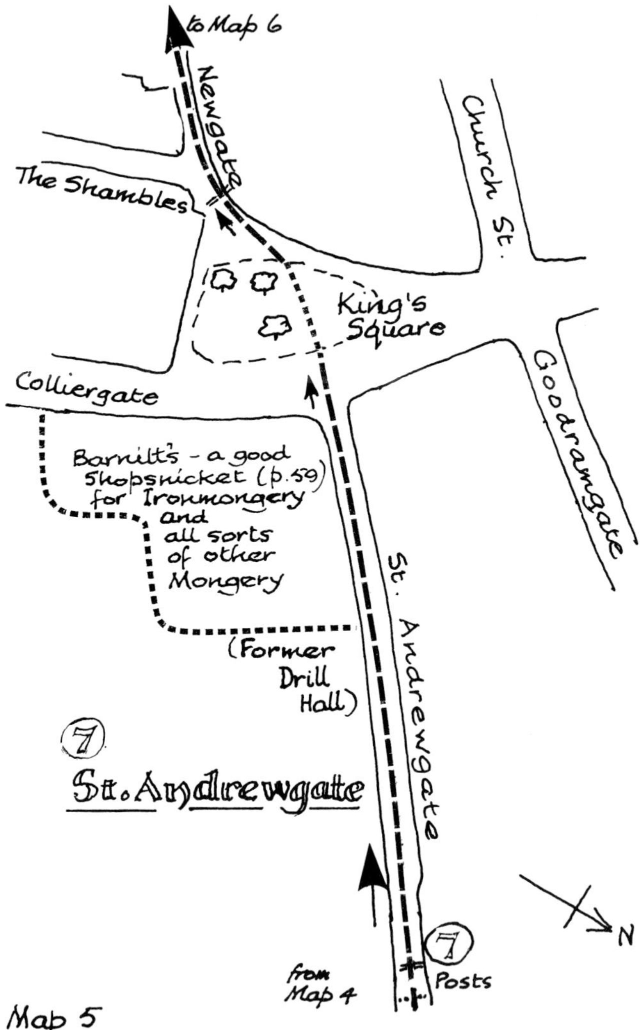

MAP 5 (St Andrewgate / King's Square)

St Andrewgate qualifies as a Snickelway solely because it boasts a row of posts at its junction with Spen Lane. By this means the York City Council bestowed upon the street the status of CYCLEWAY. It now forms part of an ever-extending network of cycleways in the city, devised primarily to protect York's large cycling fraternity from assault by motor-traffic. Unfortunately the pedestrian is prey to both. If there's one thing worse than a car horn's blast, it's to be caught in the startling slipstream of the overtaking and unheralded pedaller in full flight. We can only try to keep our wits about us in these Ways of mixed fortunes.

So we now continue nervously past, on the left, a building that could be a Byzantine temple or a Victorian public wash-house, but is neither. It used to be a drill-hall, purpose-built, as well as (according to the foundation stone) an Armoury. Unfortunately the identity of the foundation-stonelayer, and when, has been erased by the ravages of time and the slip-stream of ten thousand bicycles.

We come now into King's Square: a delightful tree-shaded triangle with an air of having been there for centuries. But this is deceptive. The square assumed its present character as recently as 1937, when the medieval Christ Church was pulled down. Long before that, it was the site of the south-east gateway of the Roman fortress; and there remains a panel of the original wall in the basement of the building on the corner of Goodramgate.

Today King's Square is usually a hive of good-natured activity. It's a natural arena for street musicians, many of them very good indeed; and there are always people around with time to stop, listen and chat on their way to and from the market and The Shambles.

Before moving on into Newgate, you may find yourself walking over a certain well-worn tombstone (if it isn't already occupied by the player of a guitar, flute or double-bass):

"Here lieth the body of the Revd. Mr. Tho. Gylby ....His known good Carracter needs no ENCOMIUMS" (My capitals)

"Whatever is an Encomium?" you may well wonder, as did I. Well, it's a sort of public tribute. One wonders therefore why they carved it, and in stone, if there was no need. "He was a good man" would have taken only half the number of "carracters". And a good man he must indeed have been: Living until the age of 97 in 1761, he had achieved more than twice man's normal life expectancy at that time.

King's Square

1993: Note that Ladies, as well as Gentlemen, are now without port-of-call in St. Sampson's Square (see page 31)

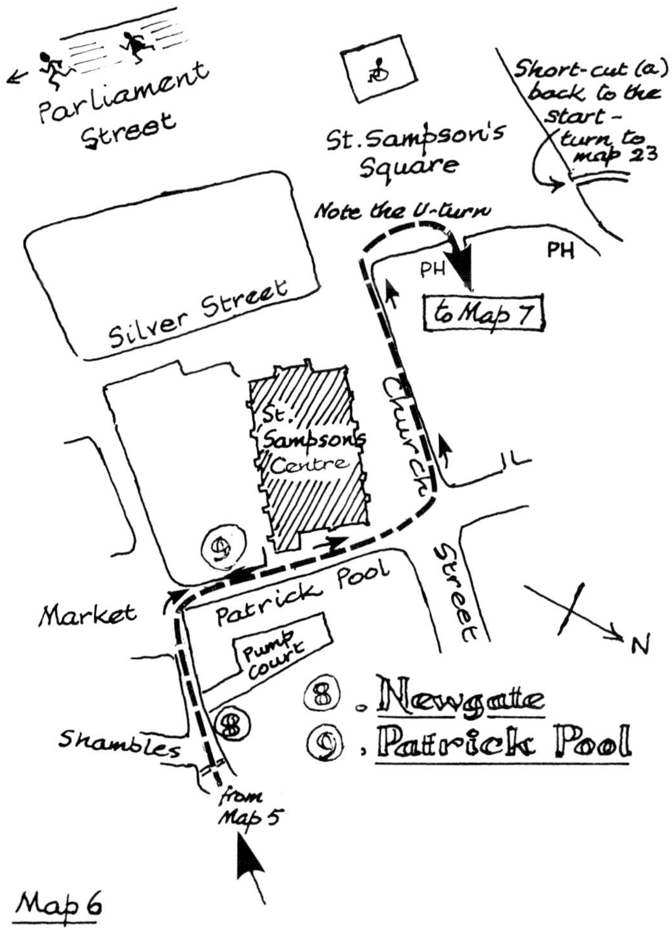

Map 6

MAP 6 (Newgate/St Sampson's Square)

On leaving King's Square, don't let yourself be sucked into The Shambles by the main current of pedestrians: that must wait until later. Carry on instead into Newgate. Almost immediately, on the right, is the secluded Pump Court, little changed since the 14th century. The name is a reminder of the former dependence of city-dwellers on the nearest water-pump or well. York's earliest Ordnance Survey map of 1851 shows 79 of them in the inner Snickelways area alone.

After passing a building in which Wesley used to preach in the 1750s, we turn right into Patrick Pool – a narrow and much-congested ancient lane. Originally named PATRICPOL in around 1200 AD., it took its name from a watery accumulation emanating from a blocked Roman sewer or a subsided Roman bath.

We now skirt St Sampson's Centre, a redundant medieval church, very successfully converted into a meeting-place for Senior Citizens. Its one draw-back is that it is served by Church Street, which we must now cross with consummate care.

Church Street is short in length,

lacking in history (it didn't exist until 1835) and devoid of real attraction. At times of vehicular access, it comes near to Anarchy Rule. Motor vehicles going north treat it as a one-way street, which it isn't. Pedestrians spill into it as though it's a permanent Foot-street. And cyclists weave a devious and determined pattern around everyone and everything, asserting their territorial rights, of which they have none.

But by keeping our wits about us, we make pretty short work of Church Street, and turn right into St. Sampson's Square. It marks the end of the first section of our walk (and indeed offers an escape-route for those who've had enough) and we take time for some reflection on the next page.

<u>It takes all sorts to make a world</u>....

Dipping into the current hefty Bartholomew's guide to York, I've come across the following reference to the territory in our next Section: It refers to "sundry linking passages where even seasoned inhabitants have occasionally to reorientate themselves, with <u>little to see</u> warranting the visitor's getting lost" (my underlining). Well, it's a free world. "Little to see"? We shall see!

Patrick Pool
(as it would be without market stalls)

Saint Sampson's Square

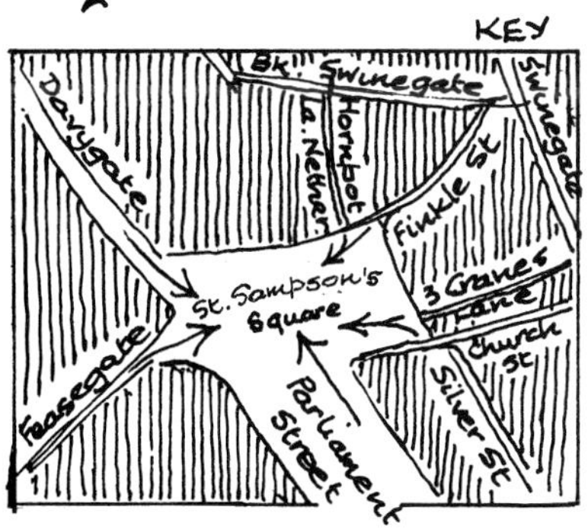

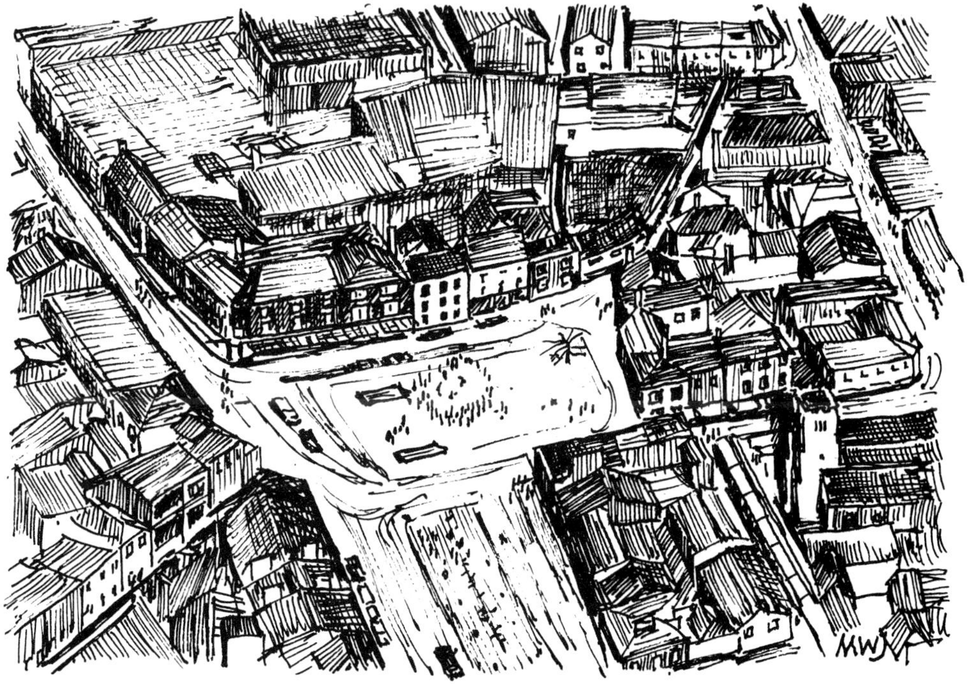

St Sampson's Square is the hub of the Snickelways, and for a simple reason: For centuries it was the Market, where people came from miles around to buy their meat, poultry, eggs and other provisions and utensils. Indeed, its real name, from around 1250, was. THURSDAY MARKET. Not until 1841 did it acquire its present title.

The short-cuts that people took to and from the market became alley-ways and streets, and account for many of our Snickelways: Finkle St, Hornpot Lane Nether, Pope's Head Alley, Silver Street and Three Cranes Lane, to name but a few.

So although St. Sampson's Square may now appear to be an adjunct to Parlia-

<u>ment Street</u>, it has a separate identity dating back much further than that of its larger neighbour. The latter was built as a new market place in 1835, and remained thus until some 20 years ago when, amid much protest, the market was exiled to its present home adjoining The Shambles and Newgate.

Perhaps because of the cavalier shunting around of the market, the number of Taverns in St Sampson's Square has shrunk from 7 in 1852 to the present 2. You will have three opportunities to visit either or both (if the time of day is right), as our route passes through the Square thrice.

[In this Square, until 1992, were to be found Conveniences for Ladies, but not for Gentlemen. But the City Council, mindful of the evils of sex discrimination, has now despatched the Ladies to join the Gentlemen at the far end of Parliament Street. For a full account of this saga, see page 56]

SECTION MAP B.

St Sampson's Square to Stonegate

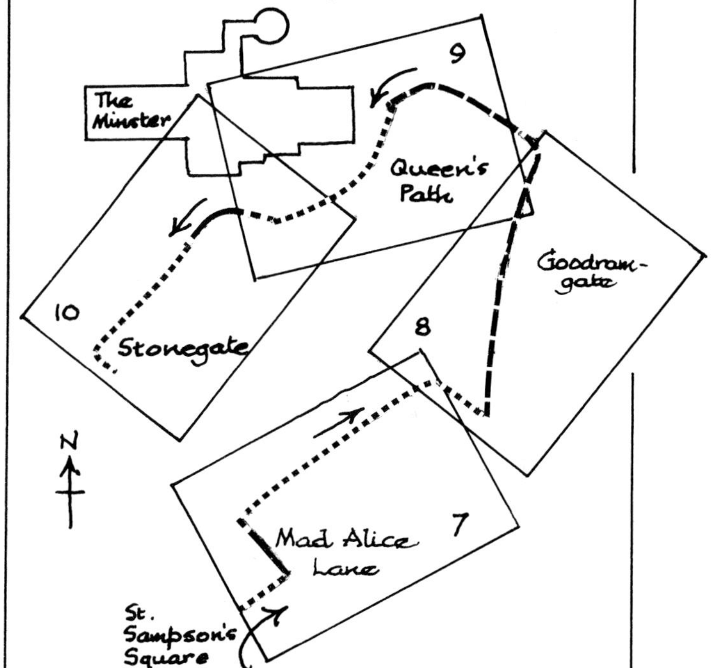

Detail maps 7 to 10

A circuitous Section embracing ten Snickelways

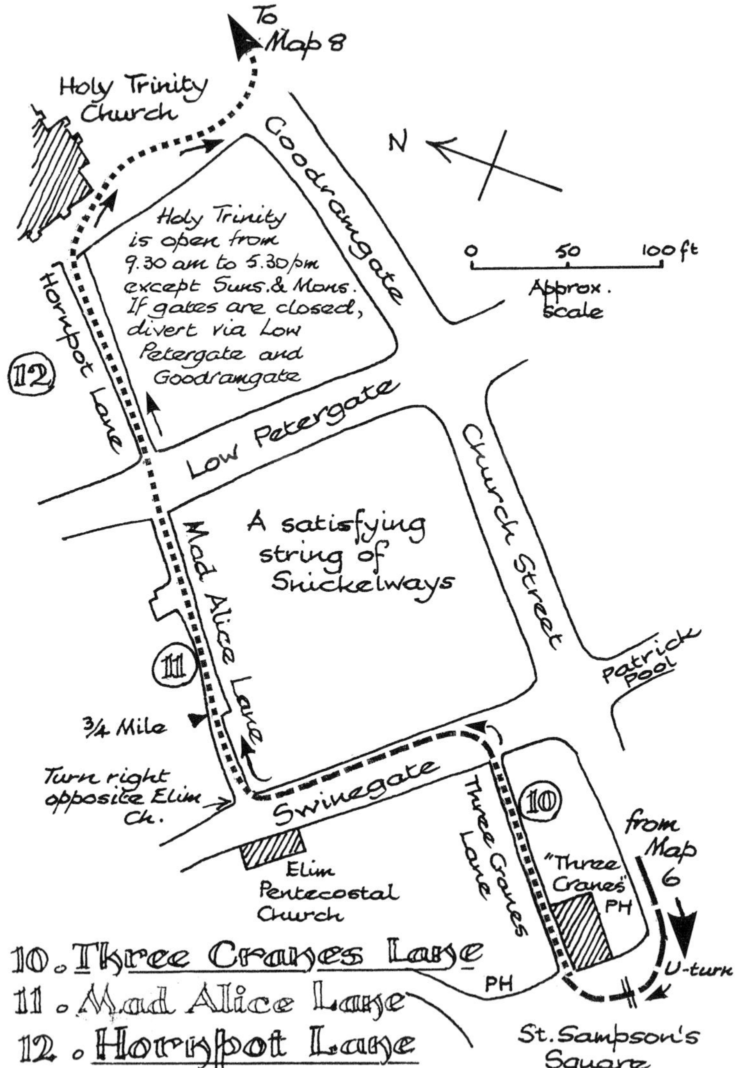

Map 7

MAP 7 (St. Sampson's Square/Hornpot Lane)

Our first encounter with St. Sampson's Square is very brief indeed: sufficient only to do a U-turn round the frontage of the "Three Cranes" before entering the tunnel of Three Cranes Lane. It isn't very prepossessing: the tunnel develops into a chasm lined with downpipes, and you'll probably find litter under your feet. But underfoot, too, are those well-trodden paving slabs, to remind you of centuries of footfalls as people came this way to and from the Market.

As for the litter: disgraceful though this is, and an indictment of our English litterloutishness, it is as much in keeping with the past as the ancient paving-slabs. The beer cans and fish-and-chip wrappings are the modern equivalent of the noisome rubbish deposited in these alleyways by our forebears, who left bones, offal and other unspeakable garbage to accumulate. But they had no disposal service: We have no excuse.

Back into the present, we come out into Swinegate and turn left. We're still not out of the old market area: Swinegate was formerly the pig-market, along with the present Back Swinegate and Little Stonegate. They formed a continuous thoroughfare, SWYNGAILL, which linked up with Patrick Pool.

After 30 yards or so, we turn right into another, rather pleasanter Snickelway leading through a miniature courtyard into Low Petergate. Some call it Lund's Court, but we prefer Mad Alice Lane – so-named because one Alice Smith lived here until 1825, when she was hanged at York Castle for being mad. The City Council has graciously granted us both alternative names on its sign (1992) at the far end.

There's no doubt whatever about the name of the next Snickelway, the entry to which is almost opposite to Lund's Court, across Low Petergate. It bears this informative plaque:

> HORNPOT LANE
>
> Leading to Holy Trinity Church
>
> A name which has survived from the late 13th Century. Excavations in 1957-58 revealed a 14th century pit in this area containing the remains of horns associated with the horn-making industry.

This information (which like all other such plaques was scrupulously researched) carefully doesn't claim that there was no other Hornpot Lane. There may have been more: Drake mentions one "between Patrick Pool and Thursday Market"; and Jeffries' map of 1773 names the Snickelway from Thursday Market to Back Swinegate as Hornpot Lane. It all adds up to a plethora of horns, pots and lanes.

The accredited Hornpot Lane is visually disappointing. But at the far end, pleasure awaits...

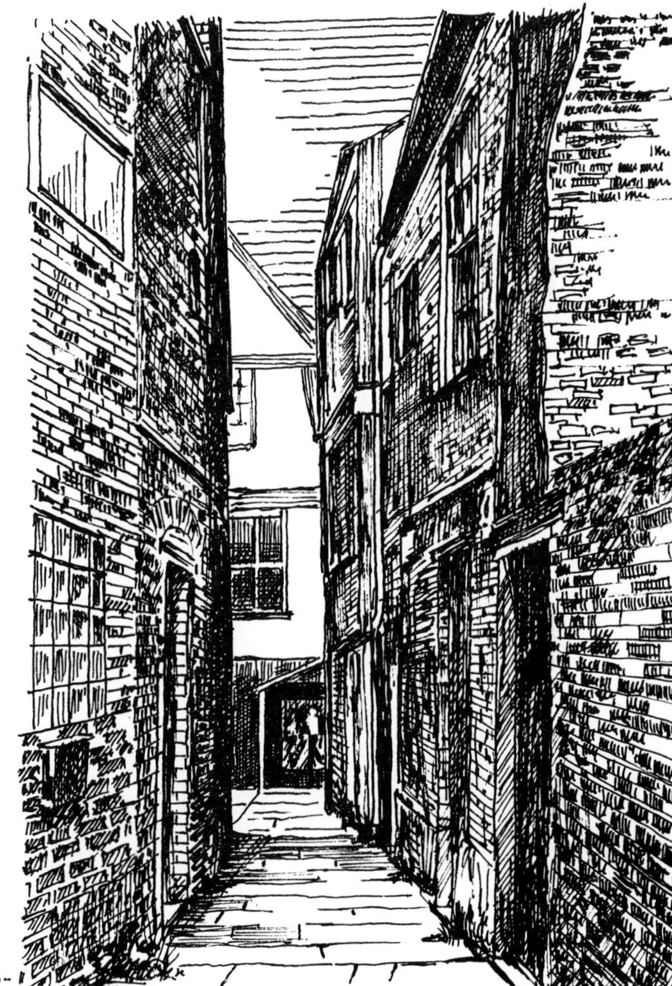

Mad Alice Lane

MWJ

The Gateway, Holy Trinity & Tonge's Court MWJ

MAP 8 (Holy Trinity to Bedern Passage)

If you didn't know until now what a HAGIOSCOPE was, then soon you will; for there's one in the intriguing little Holy Trinity Church, which awaits you at the far end of Hornpot Lane. It also possesses a saddle-back (pitched) roof to its tower; higgledy-piggledy box-pews that face in all directions; a floor that slopes this way and that; and a double-decker pulpit. Alas, no one normally preaches from the latter nowadays, as Holy Trinity, built between 1250 and 1500, is now a redundant church. But it is lovingly cared for by the Friends of Holy Trinity, open to visitors by day and floodlit by night. (By the way, that Hagioscope was a "squint-hole" – an angled opening through which the priest down in the chapel altar could keep an eye on the high altar: an early manifestation of closed-circuit viewing).

As you come out again into the daylight, you are able to savour the quietness of the secluded little churchyard. I refer to it here as Tonge's Court, so that this old name is not forever forgotten (though some say that it was an earlier name for Hornpot Lane). On the eastern side, ahead of us, are the cottages of Lady Row: York's and probably

Europe's oldest surviving houses. The world usually hurries past them on the far side, in busy Goodramgate. Here in this peaceful little close, we can absorb the atmosphere as they knew it six centuries ago.

With some reluctance we leave Tonge's Court through the gateway in the far corner, and (watching out for the traffic that shouldn't be there) cross Goodramgate. But having done so, just turn and look back at that lovely mellow brick archway. Built in 1766, with wrought iron gates added in the year of Waterloo, it usually goes un-noticed, upstaged by the adjoining Lady Row. In the sketch I've tried to bring to it - by isolation - the attention and admiration that it deserves. The gateway's modest aspirations now appear: it frames, not Holy Trinity, but the more distant and mighty West tower of the Minster!

Before finally leaving this attractive little vista, note one more curiosity: the end wall of the Lady Row cottages is at quite a sharp angle. This pattern is continued right through the row (except at the northern endmost cottage) so that every house is off-square.

And so down Goodramgate...

(Continued on page 38)

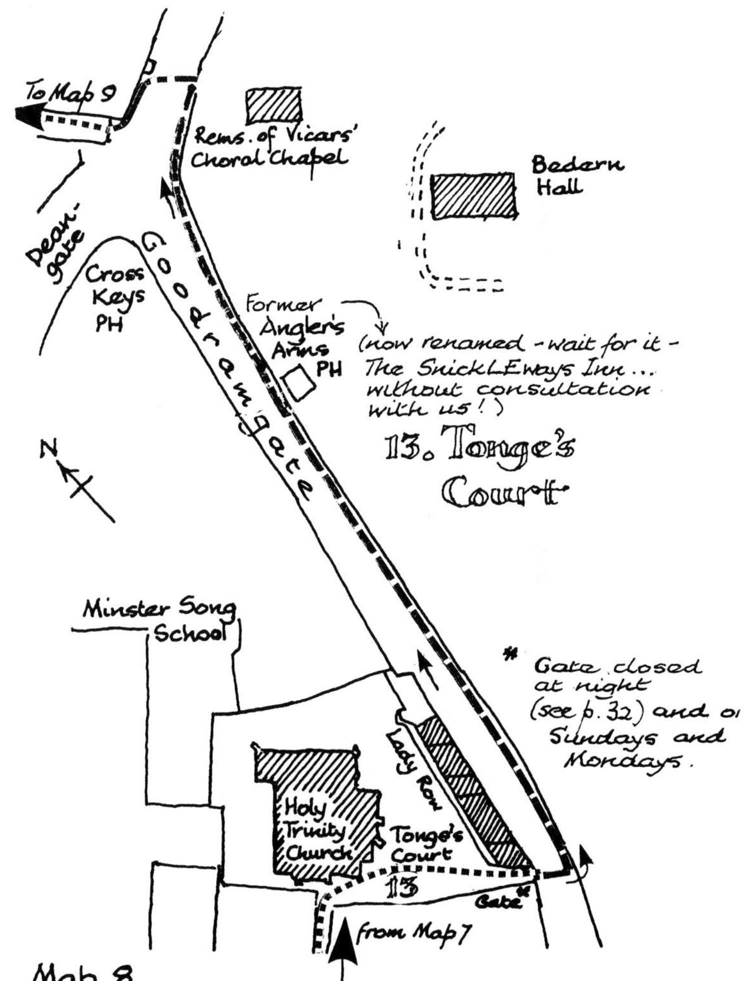

Map 8

YORK'S ENVIRONMENTAL GUARDIANS

Of all City Councils, York must have more than its share of influential organisations breathing down its neck. For this we should be thankful. York is too precious for the preservation of its character to be subject solely to local governmental judgement, however dedicated.

Not that the City Council is uncaring: far from it. With very few exceptions, post-war York has set its face against the atrocious planning decisions made elsewhere, and a sensitive Council has ensured that most of the changes in the city have been for the good. Much of the Council's work in the area of conservation and design is quiet and unsung, and is done in careful consultation with these organisations. But now and again the latter need to raise their voice, and do so. They include:

- The York Civic Trust Founded in 1946 to improve the quality of life in York – culturally and environmentally – the Trust has some 850 to 900 members, who elect its Council. Anyone can join for a modest subscription. The Trust not only campaigns: it does a host of things, ranging (see opposite) from streetlamps, through descriptive plaques, to the conversion of medieval churches and major enterprises including the restoration of Fairfax House (page 63). The Trust hands out public bouquets and brickbats, encouraging the good and chastising the bad. It also produces the most informative, artistic and entertaining Annual Report in the land.

- YAYAS (Yorkshire Architectural and York Archeological Society). Founded 1902, but its parentage goes back to 1842. Originally concerned itself with the study of church architecture. Later, under the energetic leadership of Dr. W.A. Evelyn, it campaigned vigorously in all directions against threats to the city's heritage, especially breaches of the city walls and moats. Its campaigning role has since declined, but it remains active, especially as custodian of the unequalled Evelyn collection of prints, slides and paintings of York.

- York Archeological Trust A specialist, but charitable, Trust employing paid expert staff, to organise archeological excavation and preservation in York. The biggest of its many major projects has been the Viking dig and the subsequent Jorvik Viking Centre development; the Archeological Resource Centre (p.52); and the Barley Hall project (pp. 44/45)

- Yorkshire Philosophical Society Founded 1822. More a learned than a campaigning society, but not above making its voice heard on matters of concern to it. Until 1971 it owned and cared for the Yorkshire Museum, Museum Gardens, St. Mary's Abbey and Tempest Anderson Hall. Meets regularly for lectures and visits of cultural, historical and natural history interest.

- Other voluntary organisations include the York Georgian Society (upholding all things Georgian); York 2000 (campaigning against despoilation by traffic) and the River Foss Society (cherishing every inch of its banks, flora & fauna).

- The City of York Council is not, therefore, without advice.

A characteristic lamp in the Snickelways. This one is to be found in Pope's Head Alley. There are some thirty others.

LAMPS OF THE SNICKELWAYS

If you see a graceful lamp with black paintwork, gilded crest and corners and a wrought-iron bracket, then the chances are that you're in or near to a Snickelway. Not all have them; nor are they confined to the Snickelways. But they are an essential part of the character and illumination of the Snickelways.

Not only do they illuminate in the physical sense: they are lovely examples of craftsmanship – of "making something a little better than it needs to be in order to fulfil its purpose". Compare this with the precast concrete street-light!

Their preservation and maintenance have not of course happened by accident. They are the responsibility of the City Council; but they are also one of the many concerns of the York Civic Trust, which has paid for the maintenance and gilding of many of them.

Most date back to the 1820s and the days of gas-light. Only an exceptional few are still gaslit: the remainder were converted to electricity, initially with household bulbs. But with characteristic care, the Trust and the Council have ensured their replacement (in most cases) with small, round bulbs, more akin to the shape and size of the old gas mantles, and giving a mellow light.

So by night these lamps still cast their intimate light and shadow in the Snickelways. By day, they add grace and dignity to their unpretentious and quiet surroundings.

MAP 8 (Commentary continued)

GOODRAMGATE, which we keep encountering, comes from the Danish GUTHERAN, and dates back to the 12th Century. It's a mixture of old, tasteful, new and tasteless. At this end it's supposed to be traffic-free; but beware of vehicles shouldering aside innocent pedestrians.

Between Goodramgate and Bedern / St Andrewgate, to the east, there used to be a number of medieval lanes. Unfortunately all have been absorbed into private properties, including most tantalisingly Powell's Yard — an alluring 16th century courtyard. This was indeed included, with the kind permission of the owners, as a Snickelway in the first editions of this book.

But sad to say, a small minority behaved anti-socially in Powell's Yard. Whether they were Snickellers, or customers of a nearby hostelry, is a matter for speculation. But this Yard must now be excluded from our walk and from our gaze. I can't bear however to exclude this drawing, which may give you an idea of the beauty which lies beyond the locked gate.

Powell's Yard.

Please rest content with this sketch of the forbidden fruit, in the knowledge that the pleasure of every other scene depicted in this book is still there to be shared.

A NOTE ABOUT LITTER

LITTER!...

People blame the City Engineer, the Take-away shops, the scarcity of street-cleaners, the unavailability of litter-bins — everybody but the people who actually drop the stuff! It has even been seriously suggested in the York City Council that all the seats should be removed from King's Square ....so that people won't be tempted to sit down, and won't therefore drop their litter! What a counsel of despair!

But what to do? In the short term, press for more bins; more frequent emptying; set an example and use them; show litter-droppers (politely, of course) where they are, what they're for....

But long-term, as a nation we need to educate ourselves and our children to take a pride in the tidiness of our streets (and Snickelways!). Only then shall we be able to attain the litter-free standards achieved by our friends in Scandinavia, the Netherlands, Germany, Austria, Switzerland... to name but a few.

And then, too, we might be trusted to carry on sitting in King's Square!

P.S. But see my note in the Introduction to the fifth edition....

College Street, through Bedern Arch

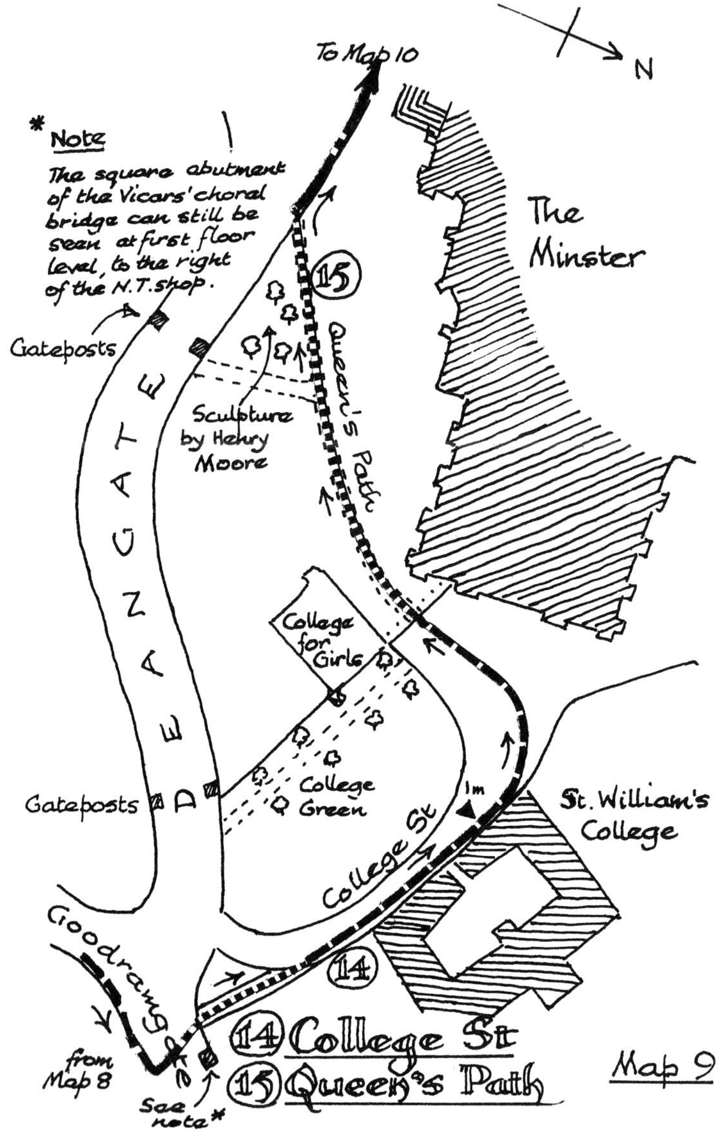

MAP 9. College Street/Queen's Path

Unlike ourselves, the Vicars Choral (no doubt singing on their way) were able to make their way unharrassed from Bedern into Vicar's Lane (now College Street); for they were provided with a flyover footbridge across Goodramgate, in 1396.* Earthbound, we now have to take our chance with the traffic. But as we pass under the timbered archway beside the National Trust shop it is easy to visualise the 15th Century scene: The Minster, as now, soaring majestically in the background, with St. William's College on the right. It was founded in 1465 to accommodate the Chantry Priests. These Chanting Priests (not to be confused with the Singing Vicars) seem to have reserved their main efforts until nightfall: they are said to have indulged in "colourful nocturnal habits". Whether or not as a consequence, this street was given another name: Little-Alice Lane.

Meanwhile the College was taken over during the Civil War by Charles I, to be used first as a printing house, and then as the Royal Mint. During the 19th century it was converted into tenements, and unbelievably the handsome timbering was completely obliterated with stucco. Not until 1906 was it restored again, since when, with further detailed restoration and imaginative floodlighting, it has surpassed itself.

We bear left now, over the cobbles, to the newer, dignified and pleasant pathway, the Queen's Path.

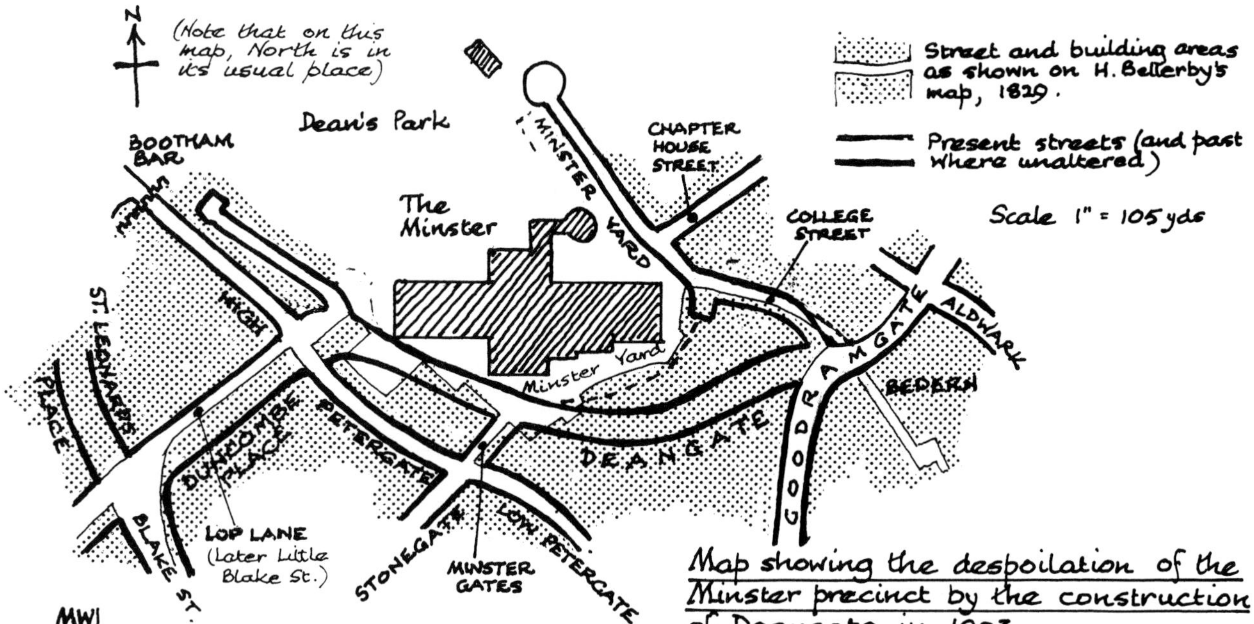

<u>Map showing the despoilation of the Minster precinct by the construction of Deangate in 1903.</u>

As we skirt the Minster along the Queen's Path, I make no apology for using this page to comment not on the Minster itself, but on its surrounds. Recalling the peace, calm and serenity of Dean's Park, it was a sad reflection that until 1989 the southern surrounds were subjected to constant reverberation. 130 years ago it was approachable only through four little streets: Chapter House and College Streets, Minster Gates and Lop Lane. Even up to 1903 it remained secluded, though the narrow Lop Lane ("flea alley") had twice been widened fairly painlessly to form Duncombe Place.

But then Deangate was created, by breaking a way through from Goodramgate to Minster Yard. It was the 1903 equivalent of driving an urban Motorway past – and virtually across – the doorstep of the Minster!

Finally, after years of pressure by the Dean and the Civic Trust, the citizens of York voted resoundingly in 1990 for the permanent closure of Deangate to traffic. Now, the blackbird sings again high above Minster gates, its song re-echoing from the Minster's walls.

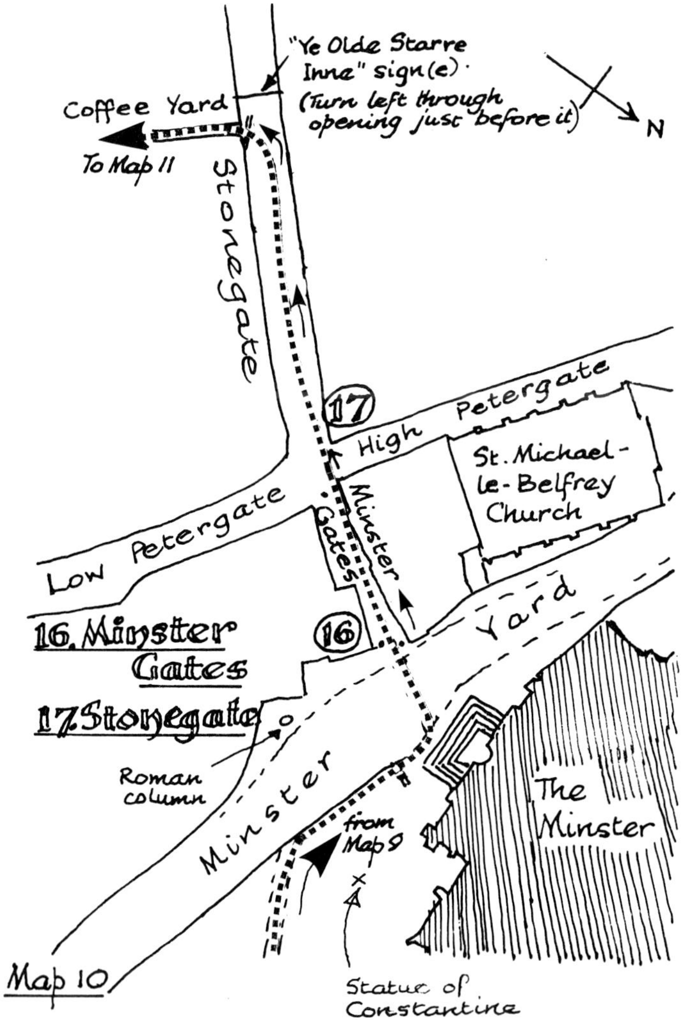

Map 10. Minster Gates & Stonegate

The roof of the Minster's South Transept, and the Rose Window, soar above us as we approach Minster Yard. Now exquisitely restored after the near-disastrous fire of 1984, they reflect the dedication and skills of the Minster's own craftsmen of the 20th century. You must of course see their work from inside.

The crossing discharges us into Minster Gates – the neck of the egg-timer through which flow ceaselessly the grains of York's summer tourist sands, on their way to and from the Minster. A plaque tells us that the posts have been there since 1370. I wonder? For the Minster was then in the midst of being built (1220 to 1490), and the stone for it was being heaved up Stonegate from the riverside. This must have been a hard enough task (20,000 tons was needed for the central tower alone) without having to manoeuvre it around obstructive posts. But then... very little to do with the building of the Minster could have been easy.

Minster Gates (or Bookbinder's Alley before the Minster's completion) is another favoured venue for street musicians, whose music accompanies you across Petergate into Stonegate. Once the *Via Praetoria* of the Roman city, since 1974 Stonegate has again become a foot-street. Crowded though it may be, especially in summer, it remains nevertheless a pleasant, cheerful and friendly mixture of history and tasteful shops, pubs and cafés. And the sounds of Stonegate are of people strolling and chatting. A good place to be! But Coffee Yard awaits...

Summer in Stonegate

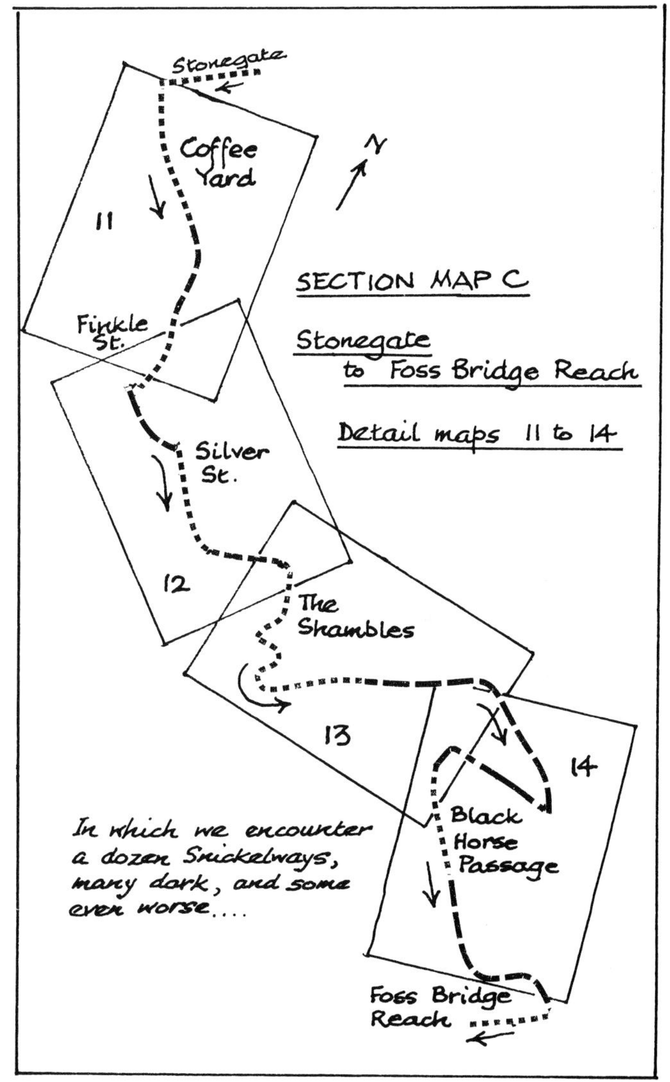

Coffee Yard, 1983

By 1992, Coffee Yard had seen meticulous restoration work by the York Archaeological Trust. Known as the Barley Hall project, it is planned to provide an insight into every-day mediaeval life. We can now enjoy William Snawsell's Town House and the former Hospice to Nostell Priory (15th & 14th century)

Beyond now lies an intriguing maze of courts and yards (Swinegate Courts), recently formed from a derelict area. Our route, however, sticks to the ancient ways.

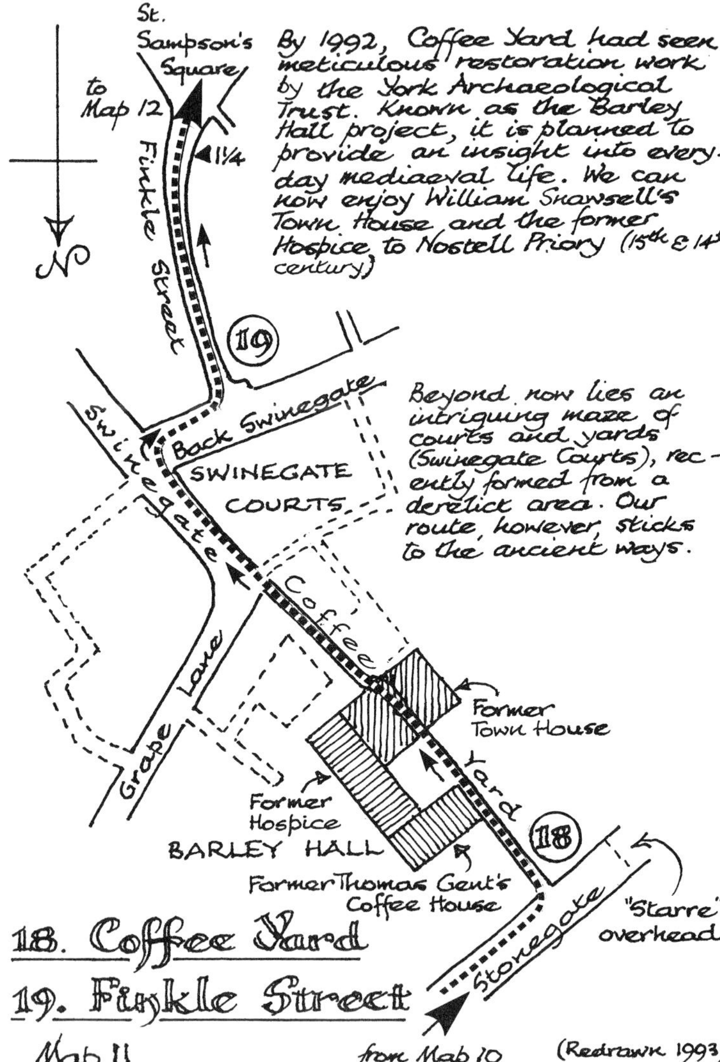

18. Coffee Yard
19. Finkle Street

Map 11

(Redrawn 1993)

MAP 11: Coffee Yard to Finkle Street

COFFEE YARD: The very quintessence of the Snickelways! It has virtually everything:
- It's very old (a Medieval Common lane)
- It's very low (minimum headroom 5'10")
- It's very narrow in places (minimum width 2'11")
- It's very long (nearly 220 feet)
- It has three tunnels, a yard and a ginnel.
- It traverses the Barley Hall project

Throw in all of these, plus its possession of a devil at one end and a four-letter word at the other, and what more could you ask of Coffee Yard? You find the Red Devil on the left of Stonegate, marking the start of Coffee Yard, in which York's first newspaper (with the aid of a Printer's Devil) was printed in 1719. Next comes Thomas Gent's Coffee House (with its roasting-oven in the cellar), followed by the buildings of Barley Hall, restored by the York Archaeological Trust (see below).). Now you're into the middle tunnel, dog-legged and with walls at all angles. Walk 18 yards along an open ginnel, and you come to the last tunnel, terminating in a real head-clouter, the lowest overhead beam in all the Snickelways. In the 14th Century, when a man's stature was less, this must have mattered little compared with what was to follow: for Grape Lane, into which we emerge, was then a street of iniquity. Francis Drake in 1736 wrote long sentences preparing his readers for Grape Lane's original name because (he wrote) "our anceſtors uſed to call a ſpade a ſpade". But then he hid it away in the midst of a Latin appendix! Not so the Royal Commission on Historic Monuments. Its name was, they forthrightly declare, Grapcunt Lane, and Grap was for grope, not grape.

Shouldering our ſpades, we march on for a few yards down Swinegate, turn right then quickly left into Finkle Street. Its 14th Century name was Finclegayle, meaning simply Angle Street. But what's this? *"It was later called Mucky Peg Lane"*! Rather than stop for another exercise in etymology, I will hustle you on round the bend, and we find ourselves back in our old friend, the Thursday Market.

This sketch is largely conjectural. It's hard to see much above first-floor level from Coffee Yard without getting a crick in your neck.

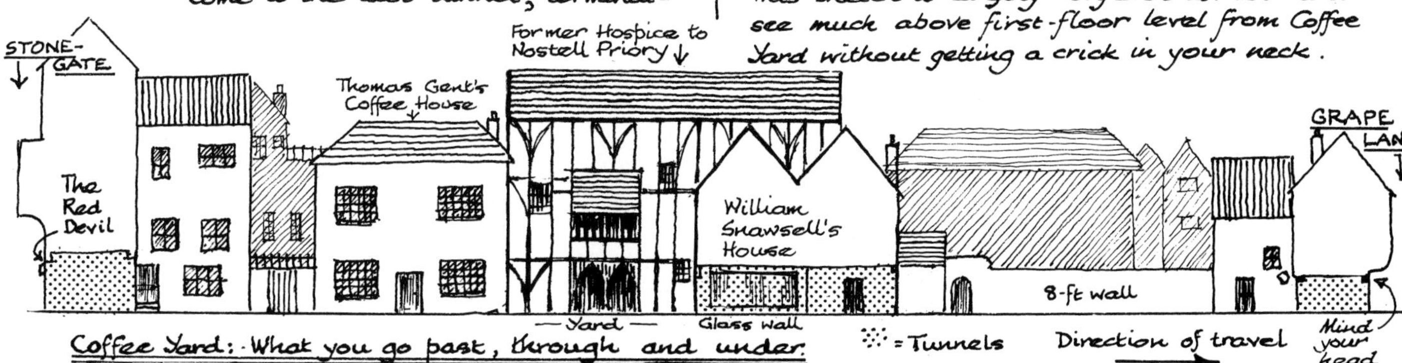

Coffee Yard: What you go past, through and under

(Revised 1993)

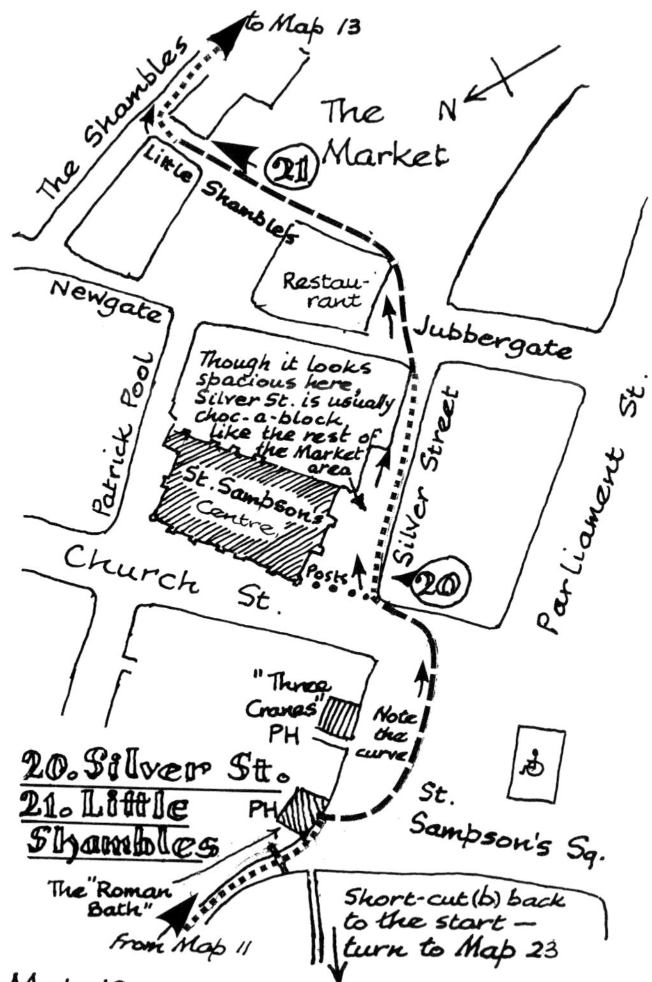

Map 12

MAP 12. St Sampson's Square again, & The Market.

Strange, how different St. Sampson's Square looks and feels from this corner, compared with our first arrival from the Church St. quarter! Perhaps it's the sudden contrast with the narrow and overshadowed streets and alleys in which we've been ever since leaving the Minster. Somehow, the Square now seems more spacious, and to have more of the air of a market square, as it was for centuries.

But before traversing it again we have an important call to pay at the pub on our left, The Roman Bath. If it isn't opening time, then you must come back when it is (even if you haven't a thirst!). For inside is surely the most ancient, fascinating and imaginatively-displayed spectacle to be found in any public bar in the kingdom: literally, a roman bath. Not just a bath for one, or even two, but a vast stone-built installation, the father of all saunas and Turkish baths, built and used as only the Romans knew how, 1900 years ago. (As you sit at your table,* you look right down into the brilliantly flood-lit excavation. It looks as though it's ahead of you – until you realise that, thanks to the inspired use of mirrors, what you can see is actually underneath you.)

*You must now (1999) go downstairs to view it, but it's well worth the small charge.

York Market

into Silver Street. As you might expect, it was the street of the silversmiths in medieval times. It also housed the York Police Station from 1841 to 1892, when they moved into their brand-new premises (now abandoned) in Clifford St. Nowadays it's where York Market starts, and our progress from here round to Little Shambles will be sporadic.

If we need a reminder that York is essentially a market town surrounded completely by richly farmed countryside, then the Market provides it. Not only do those fresh vegetables, eggs, poultry, flowers and farm butter come from places personally known to the shoppers – the smallholdings, nurseries and villages of the Vale of York; but in social terms, everybody seems to know everybody else. The market is as much a place for a good chat as a good buy (and there's an abundance of both). It's lively, congested, colourful, chaotic, cheerful and companionable.

When we leave The Roman Bath, we have an unassailable excuse for not progressing in a straight line towards Silver Street: our "no back-tracking" rule requires that we move in a gentle curve, sufficient only to take us clear of the Three Cranes, round which we U-turned six maps ago. (That is, unless you wish to pack up and go home, in which case retreat into Hornpot-Lane-Nether.)

The rest of us, having evaded the Morris-men and organ-grinders who frequent the Square in summer, must now cross Church St.

So our progress round to The Shambles is slow. If you're sorry to leave the market, don't worry. We haven't nearly finished with it yet.

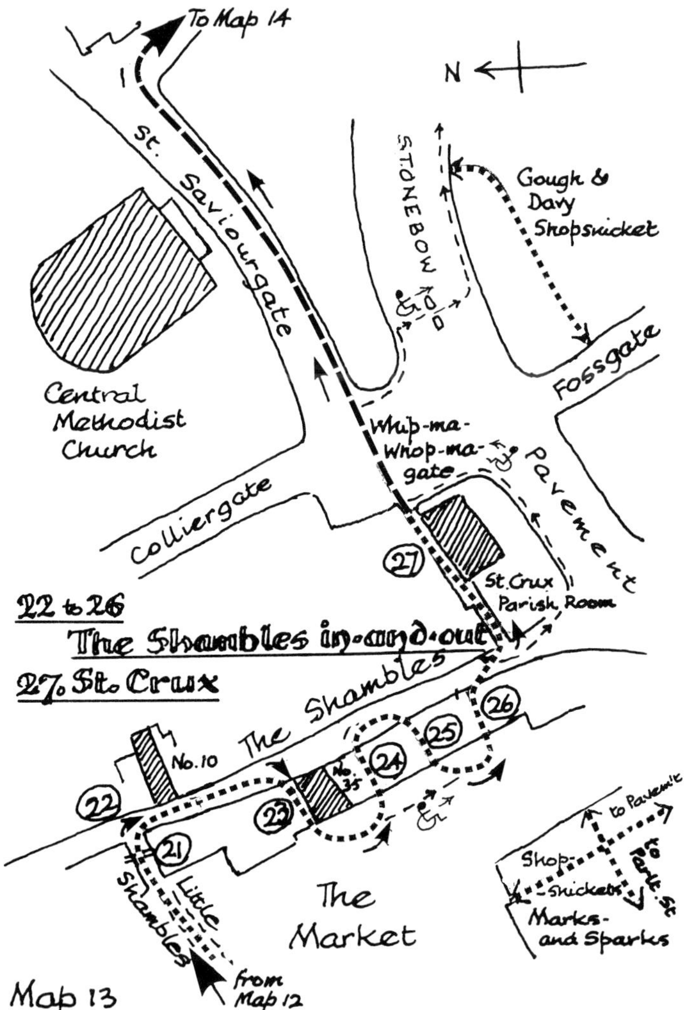

MAP 13 (The Shambles In-and-Out)

We are now poised to embark upon the Grand Slalom of the Snickelways: the Great Shambles In-and-Out. So gather your party together in Little Shambles; tell them you'll all meet up later seven Snickelways hence in Whipmawhopmagate; and consign them to every-man-for-himself. Then you're off, through the Little Shambles starting-gate.

From here, the people passing the street-end look like actors on a narrow stage, coming and going from somewhere in the wings. Not until you join them does the stage-set suddenly reveal itself as The Shambles, in all its dimensions. Even then, the overhanging houses still look at first sight like elaborate backdrops, waiting to be hauled heavenwards by stagehands hidden in the market. But no: The Shambles – or Great Shambles – is firmly set, here in the heart of York, and has been for centuries.

It has however undergone a number of name-changes: HAYMONGERGATE in 1240, then NEDLERGATE, then THE FLESHAMMELS (the street of the Butchers) finally shortened, by 1500, to The Shambles. For centuries it remained the butchers' street, with the meat hanging from the hooks above the windows and displayed on the shelves below. As late as 1830, there were still 25 butchers' shops in this street, out of a total of 88 in the whole of York.

In 1586, the wife of one young butcher, Margaret Clitherow, was found guilty of hiding a Jesuit priest, and was pressed to death under a door heaped with stones. She was canonised in 1970, and the house attributed to her - No. 35 - has been turned into a shrine. (Actually, according to the Royal Commission, her house was No. 10, now a gift shop on the opposite side).

Immediately before No. 35, a timbered arch opens up on the right, and (by now instinctively) we advance into it, to find ourselves at once back in the Market. But this time we see things through the stallholders' eye. You have a right to be here, but are not encouraged, for you are now behind the stalls. You may find yourself mistaken for a seller of vegetable marrows, bolts of cloth or crockery seconds. So better to turn left and move on quickly to the next passageway (Snickelway 24), which deposits you back into The Shambles. Ignoring the surprise of other pedestrians, who thought they'd seen the last of you, you rejoin them for a few yards before cutting back into the Market through another passageway, immediately after house No. 32. Go left again on emerging (again avoiding would-be market customers) and then, with a final flourish, enter the

The Shambles MWJ

Back-cloth for the Great Shambles In-and-Out

The twenty-third Snickelway (Shambles In-and-out)

MAP 13 (Contd.) (Shambles/St. Saviourgate)

wide finishing-gate beside Cox's shoe-repairing shop, which lands you back into The Shambles for the last time.

> If at this stage you feel the need to explain your apparent eccentricity to other citizens, show them this book. It's the only rational explanation for totally irrational behaviour.

Not that you'll have long for explanations; for after a few more yards of The Shambles, you shoot off again - this time to the left, into the passageway next to Mollie Coates' flower shop. It takes you past St. Crux parish room. This is the only vestige of the former St Crux Church - demolished in 1887 -, which used to dominate the Pavement scene from medieval times. The remaining building accommodates many of the precious artefacts that were saved from the church.

After squeezing through the narrowest gap in the Snickelways (caused by an excessively restrictive post, wholly inconsistent with the thoughtfully-ramped steps which follow) we come out into York's shortest street, which also boasts the longest word : Whip-ma-whop-ma-gate. Some have it that this eloquent-sounding name has something to do with the punishment of tiresome 16th-century wives. Well, believe that if you like. A more authentic explanation is that it derives from WHIT-NOUR-WHAT-NOUR-GATE, a Medieval expression of scorn, meaning roughly CALL-THAT-A-STREET-YOU-MUST-BE-JOKING!

By now your friends (if you have any left) should all have been disgorged from the Shambles Inandout. Gather them together, and revive them with the straight and uneventful stroll down St. Saviourgate. It seems unbelievable that from 1368 until the 1950s, this quiet street formed part of the only through route from Ouse Bridge to Layerthorpe (that is, until the advent of The Stonebow, with which we will not defile this page). St Saviourgate shared with The Shambles the preoccupation with butchery: its original name was KETMONGER-GATE, or "flesh-sellers' street".

On our left is the former Wesleyan-Methodist Centenary Chapel, built in 1840 to mark the centenary of Methodism. In contrast with the building in Newgate where Wesley preached 85 years earlier (Map 6), this vast church, looking more like a Greek temple than a chapel, was built to hold 1,500 people. From 1983 it has become the main Methodist church in the city.

On our right is a pseudo-Snickelway, for use only in case of ~~emergency~~.

St. Crux Passage, Whip-ma-whop-ma-gate

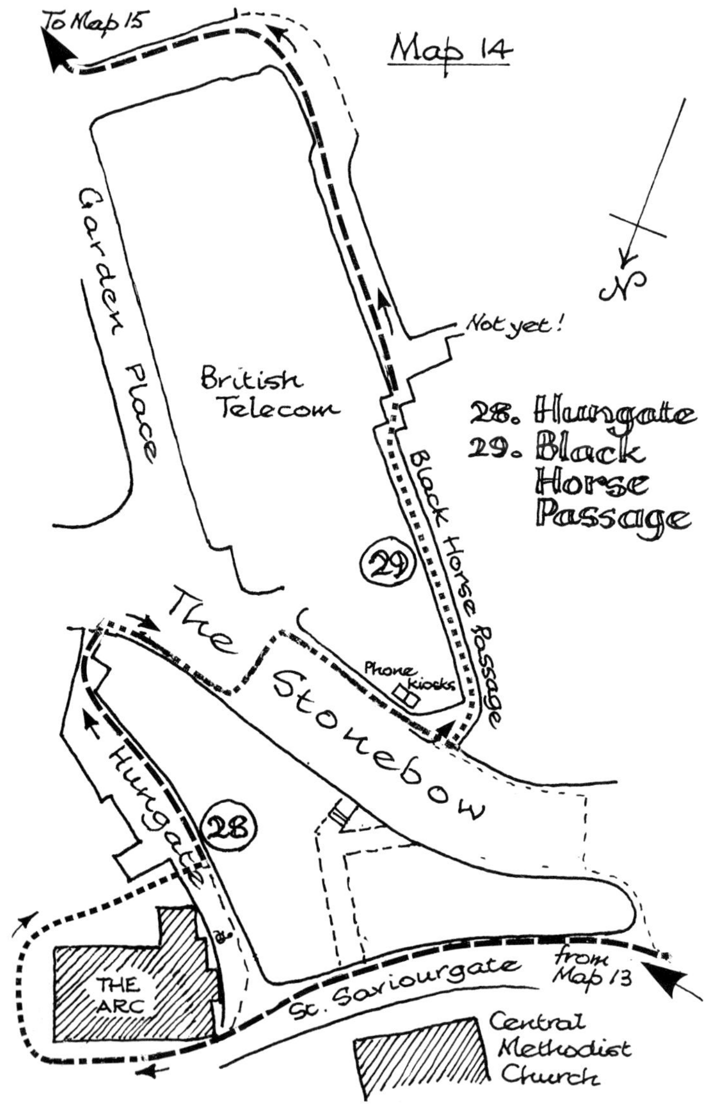

MAP 14 (Hungate to Garden Place)

Part of The ARC (and its ugly neighbour)

Ahead on the right is the former St. Saviour's Church, now converted into THE ARC: the York Archaeological Trust's Archaeological Resource Centre. Call in for an exciting insight into the fascinations of "hands-on" archaeology, before encircling the building through its little churchyard (when unlocked). Emerging, turn left down Hungate (formerly Hundegate-in-Marsch) which once ran right down to the Foss. Dank slums have been cleared, but in their place were constructed, in the 1950s, York's ugliest thoroughfare, The Stonebow; and its ugliest building, which presides over the scene. So now the truncated remnant of upper Hungate leads us abruptly from the mellow stonework of St. Saviour's into the soulless angularity of a concrete carpark ramp. At the far end, recently-erected pipe rails enforce an awkward and undignified exit, right into The Stonebow. Eyes screwed and teeth clenched, we press on until we are opposite a pair of telephone kiosks on the far side of the street. Choosing our moment, we hasten across and take refuge beyond the kiosks.

Until recent improvements by the Joseph Rowntree Foundation, we would next have encountered an unkempt cleft leading into a wilderness of vegetation. But all is not what it seems. For this is the <u>Black Horse Passage</u>, another ancient alley; and a stretch of stone wall on the right (surmounted by Victorian brick) is the remains of the wall of a Carmelite Priory. The wall was later to provide concealment for Victorian clients on their way to and from the notorious red-light area that Hungate and its surrounding streets had then become.

Black Horse Passage pre-1990

Suddenly we emerge from the former Black Horse jungle, and skirt the enormous and impressive brick-and-glass <u>British Telecom</u> building, then turn left and right into the misleadingly-named <u>Garden Place</u>, now utterly devoid of vegetation.

All-in-all, our journey across this page has not been a picturesque one. But now we are over the worst of the Snickelways walk. In a moment, a new Section — and what contrast!

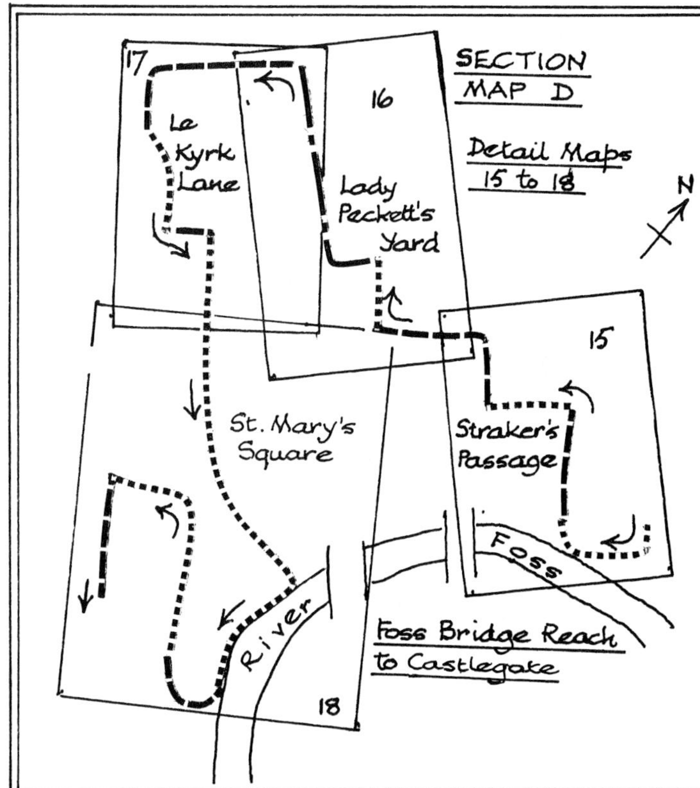

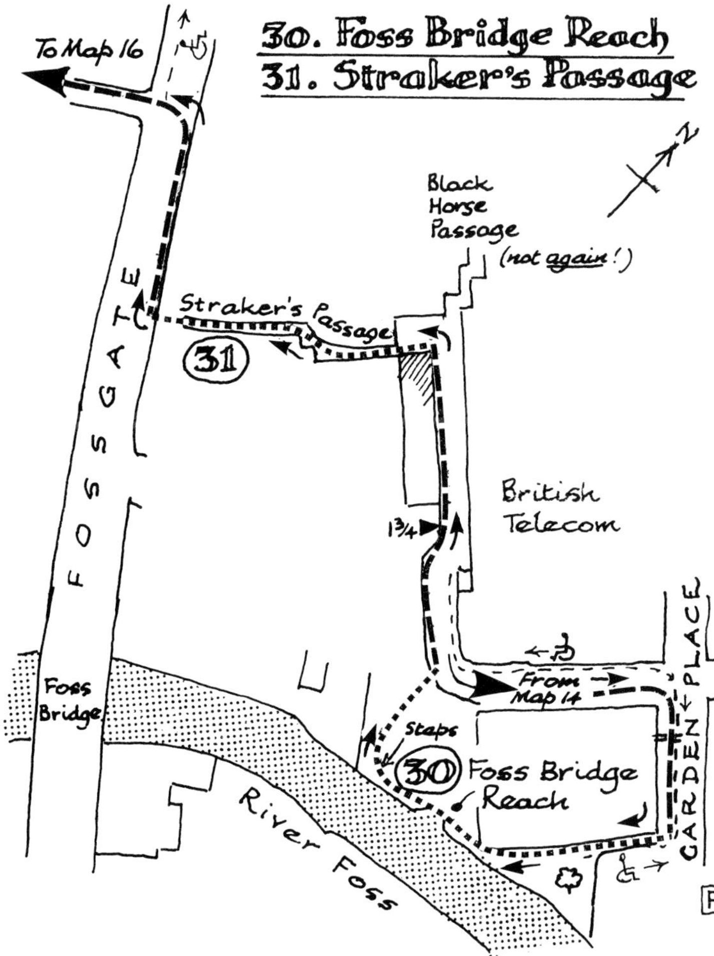

Map 15

MAP 15: Foss Bridge Reach, Straker's Passage

At the end of Garden Place is the entrance to a vast new multi-storey car park (open weekdays to 6.30 pm, pay-on-return). To avoid entrapment, turn right just before it – and suddenly you are beside the River Foss. Ahead, this little river makes its placid way under the practical but ornamental Foss Bridge, built in 1812 on the site of its lower-arched predecessor. Canal-lovers will at once feel at home here, as well they might: for this is the Foss Navigation, which from around 1800 provided a 13-mile navigable waterway, with nine locks, from York to Sheriff Hutton Bridge, north of Strensall.

Only a mile of navigation remains, but the Foss here retains its waterway atmosphere. Looking upstream, you can see the magnificent 19th century turreted building, now known as Rowntree Wharf, standing on its promontary between the river on the left and Wormald's Cut (dug in 1794) on the right. This building, originally part of a flour mill, was later used by Rowntree's as a warehouse for ingredients and materials, shipped up from Hull docks. It was acquired by the Rowntree Foundation in 1987, for use as offices and apartments (p. 86)

Our path now takes us along an attractively-designed area for contemplation, with seats and weeping-willow. As it has no name and deserves one, I refer to it here as Foss Bridge Reach. It terminates near some steps up to the right, where with some reluctance we leave this unique little canal-side corner of York.

Keeping carefully to our left to avoid our earlier footsteps, we pass again the telephone exchange, advancing almost into the jaws of the Black Horse before discovering, leading off to the left, an altogether more amiable Snickelway, Straker's passage. But although more kempt than its formerly unkempt neighbour, Straker's shares the same shady past. It takes us now unexpectedly past the back-door of the Barbican bookshop, and on into Fossgate.

For centuries this street used to be part of the main – and indeed the only – North/South route through York. The Roman route ran slightly to the east to a ford over the Foss; but Fossgate came into its own in the 14th century when the river was bridged. The bridge later accommodated not only a sea-fish market, but also a chapel, 3 shops and 23 tenements! No wonder it needed replacing.

Turning right up Fossgate, we pass the elaborate facade of the former Electric Cinema – now a furniture shop – before turning left up a street marked "Lady Peckitt's Yard". But as we shall see, this title is a bit premature.

(Continued on page 58)

Foss Bridge, from Foss Bridge Reach (1982) MWJ

Straker's Passage
(page 55)

A SAGA OF INCONVENIENCE

As we draw nearer to Parliament Street, we address an issue of injustice encountered on pages 28 & 31:

Before 1927 there stood side-by-side in Silver Street a matching but delapidated set of conveniences for Ladies and for Gents. The Council wisely decided to replace them with more seemly accommodation; and with conventional courtesy moved the Ladies first – to a site above the ground, almost slap in the middle of St. Sampson's Square.

This provoked such a hullabaloo that the Council was forced literally to back down, and to sink the Ladies' below the ground. This done, it was the turn of the Gents'; and the Council, with the wisdom of experience, confidently began to sink the Gents' alongside the Ladies. But down among the diggings was revealed an ancient sewer: *the Romans had beaten them to it.*

A second outcry arose, this time from the conservationists. By now the beleaguered Council must have been desperate (as indeed are countless men today) at having no Gents' in St. S. Square. With mounting desperation they sought any other place where a Gents' could be sunk without interfering with the Romans or anybody else. In the end they found somewhere, but not until they had reached the uttermost end of Parliament Street.

Finally, in 1992, in the light of Equal Opportunities legislation, the Council uprooted the Ladies from St. Sampson's Square, and deposited them above the distant Gents in Parliament St, now surmounted by a clock tower.

SOME OTHER NAMES for SOME SNICKELWAYS

People always did, still do, and forever will, argue about the names of Snickelways. Some of these alternative names are included in the text, and are (I believe) authentic. The others have been put forward subsequently by readers, and some may be less authentic. The possibilities, authentic or otherwise, are assembled here for you to take your pick, or add your own.

NAME USED IN THIS BOOK (In order of appearance)	ALTERNATIVE(S)
Hole-in-the-Wall	Peculiar Lane (*Peculiar = "Exempt parish"*)
Chapter House Street	Via Decumana (*Authentic Roman; not a tramcar route*)
Ogleforth	Owl's Ford: Ugel's Ford
Penny Lane	St. Andrew's Passage; Weeping Dog Lane
St. Andrewgate	Ketmongergate (*according to some, but not the R. Commission. See St. Saviourg'te*)
Patrick Pool	Patricpol
Mad Alice Lane	Lund's Court; Waiting Women's Lane
Tonge's Court	Holy Trinity Churchyard (*Tonge's Court was hereabouts*)
Lady Peckett's Yard	Bacusgail; Bakehouse Lane
College St.	Vicar's Lane; Little Alice Lane (*a different Alice*)
Minster Gates	Bookbinder's Alley
Coffee Yard	Langton Lane (*after a Lord Mayor*); Pressgang Lane
Finkle Street	Mucky Peg Lane; M. Pig Lane
The Shambles	Haymongergate; Nedler Gate; Fleshammels
St. Crux Passage	Whip Dog Lane (*a different dog*)
St. Saviourgate	Ketmongergate (*according to R. Commission*)
Hungate	Hundegate-in-Marsch; Bog-dog Lane (*yet a further dog*)
Cheat's Lane	Trichour (*Trickster's*) Lane; Lady Peckitt's Yard (south)
Le Kyrk Lane	Peter-Lane-Little; Little Thief Lane; Pope's Head Alley (1852 map)
Pope's Head Alley	Thief Lane; Intro Lane (*a means of forced introduction to a stranger*)
Hornpot-Lane-Nether	Bull Passage (*After "The Bull" PH formerly hereabouts*)

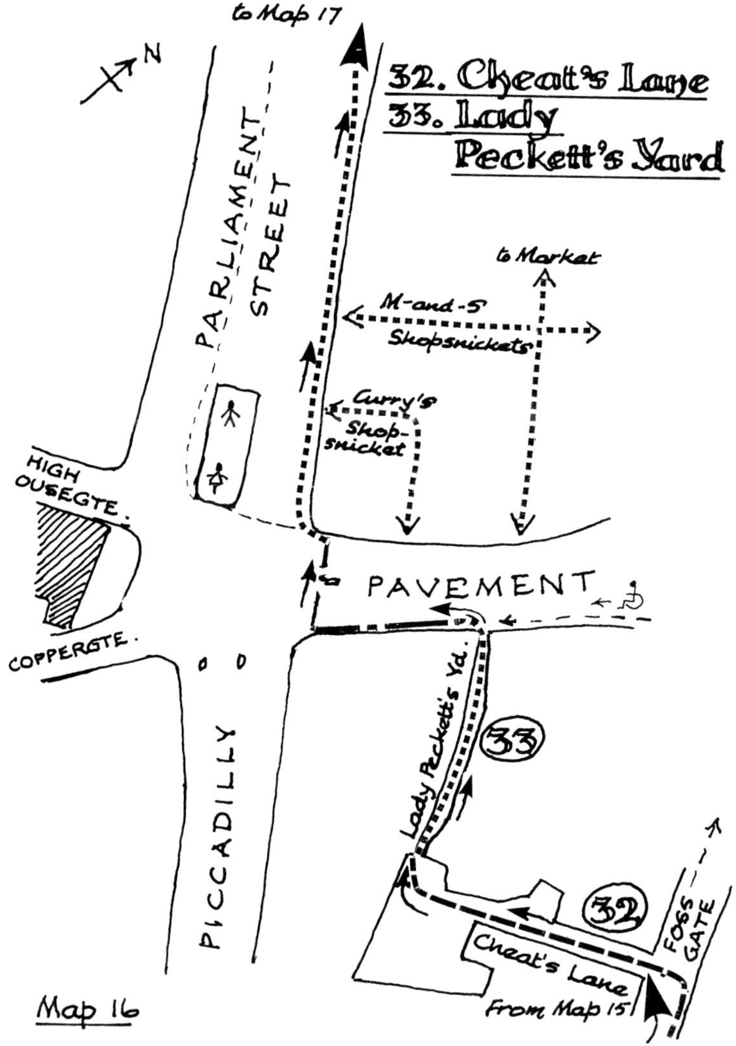

Map 16

MAP 16 : Cheat's Lane to Parliament St.

We have now turned left out of Fossgate into what is signed "Lady Peckett's Yard". However, I've shown this unprepossessing place as Cheat's Lane: first because it seems to be cheating to call it a Snickelway at all; second, because it is not the real Lady Peckett's Yard; and third, because its real medieval name was Trichour Lane, or Trickster's Lane, or – believe it or not – Cheat's Lane. It is now a sort of backyard to a pub and a nightclub.

Go straight on towards what looks like a dead-end in the far right hand corner – and Lo! You're back in medieval times! The lovely old alleyway that opens up suddenly on your right is the real Yard of Lady Peckett. Not only did she remain a Lady for the rest of her life for being the wife of a sometime Lord Mayor (who was never a Lord): but she also succeeded in having this Yard re-named after her, although since 1312 it already had a perfectly good name: Bacusgail, or Bakehouse Lane. In ascending its steps, you will also pass a CORDWAINER'S. (Any guesses?). It's a fine example of the Conservation Trust's properties and restorations.

We come out into Pavement, and this also had another name: in 1086 it was Marketshire, before achieving its present name in 1329, as it was probably the first paved street in the city. On our left as we join it was the original Rowntree's grocer's shop.

We now have to cross the end of Pavement at the traffic lights: they control its intersection with Coppergate, Parliament Street and Piccadilly, but for most of York's history there was no crossroads here at all. Pavement was linked direct with Coppergate, with the line of buildings on our left continuing straight across, and there was once a market and market-cross north of All Saints'.

Entering Parliament Street, we note a recent ornate, pillared building on our left, whose vital purpose is conveyed by minuscule figures on its modest entrance doors. [See pages 31, 56]

Thereafter we continue among the fountains until we reach Jubbergate (on the next map).

A Note on SHOPSNICKETS

A Shopsnicket is a way through a shop from one street to another. It is not of course a right-of-way, and can't be a Snickelway. Having said which, I've marked some in case you find them useful. The rule is simply to behave as a normal prospective customer (which of course you are). It is foul play to enter a Shopsnicket without an interest in its wares nor means to purchase them, or in a group of more than two (well... three).

Lady Peckett's Yard

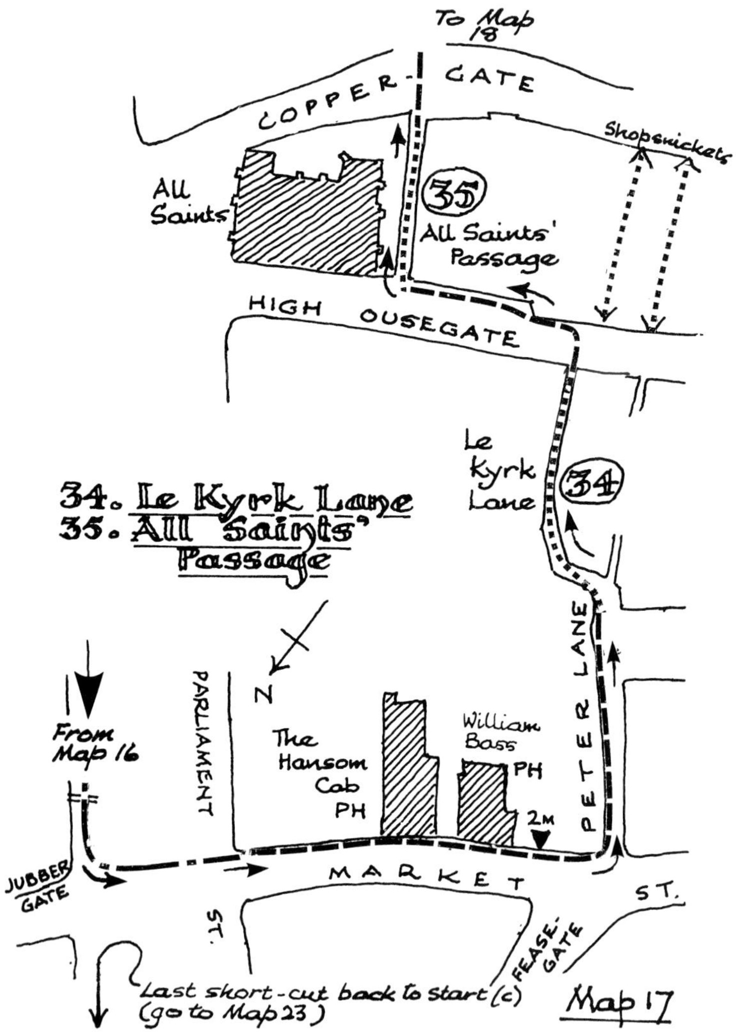

Map 17: Parliament St. to All Saints

It's worth stopping for a moment on the corner of Jubbergate, to imagine it as it was originally, before Parliament Street was built in the 1830s. It then included the present Market Street, and ran right through to Coney Street. Its name was just about as long: JOUBRETTEGAT, meaning no less than "The-Street-of-the-Bretons-in-the-Jewish-Quarter." We now follow its old line across Parliament Street, pausing again amid the cycle-racks in the middle, this time to picture the great Street-Market that used to be here. Five continuous rows of stalls stretched all the way from Pavement to St. Sampson's Square: Put end-to-end, they'd have extended for over half a mile. In sheer floorspace alone, this market would have outdone many a supermarket.

Once into Market Street, we pass in rapid succession two pubs. The first, "The Hansom Cab", is a reminder that this one-horse carriage was actually invented in York by a Micklegate architect, Joseph Hansom. Unlike "The Roman Bath", this pub doesn't contain a display of its subject matter (you'll have to call in at the Castle Museum for that).

Lulled into unawareness by recent open

streetscapes, it's easy to be unprepared for what follows. Turning left into the cramped Peter Lane, we now advance towards a narrowing funnel of girders, fall-pipes, fire escapes and fish-and-chip papers. This in turn becomes two dark clefts amid towering cliffs of Victorian brickwork, of which we take the left-hand one. It curves and gets ever-narrower, so that passing anyone else becomes a painstaking and intimate process. For this is Le Kyrk Lane, or Peter-Lane-Little. No Victorian upstart, it was a well used Medieval Common Lane, thus called because it led to the former church of St. Peter-de-Little, which abutted onto the left-hand wall. With such restricted access, its congregation must have been slow to arrive and even slower to depart – as we now must, into the relative spaciousness of High Ousegate.

Crossing and turning left, we come to All Saints' Church. Again, all is not what it seems: Apart from its title (All-Saints'-Pavement, when it isn't in Pavement at all) the lovely lantern-tower is only a 19th-century replica of the 15th Century original. But this in no way detracts from its impressiveness. Floodlit against the night sky, this prominent landmark is a continuing reminder of the lantern-tower's purpose: to guide travellers stumbling at night towards York, through forest and marsh. As for us, our path lies down the short All Saints' passage, towards yet another transition in time...

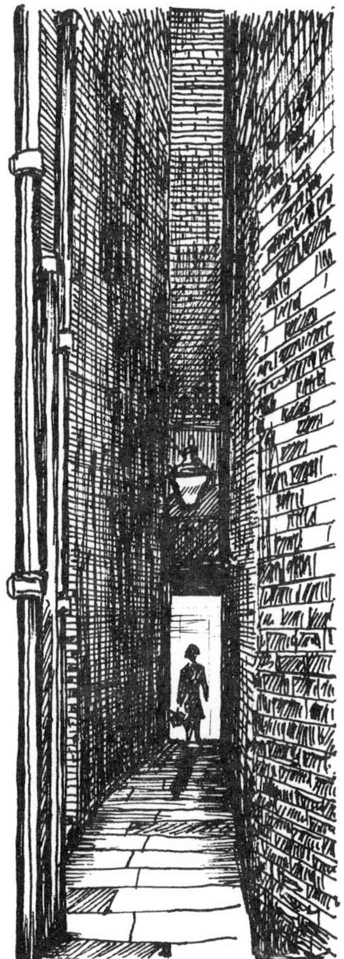

Le Kyrk Lane

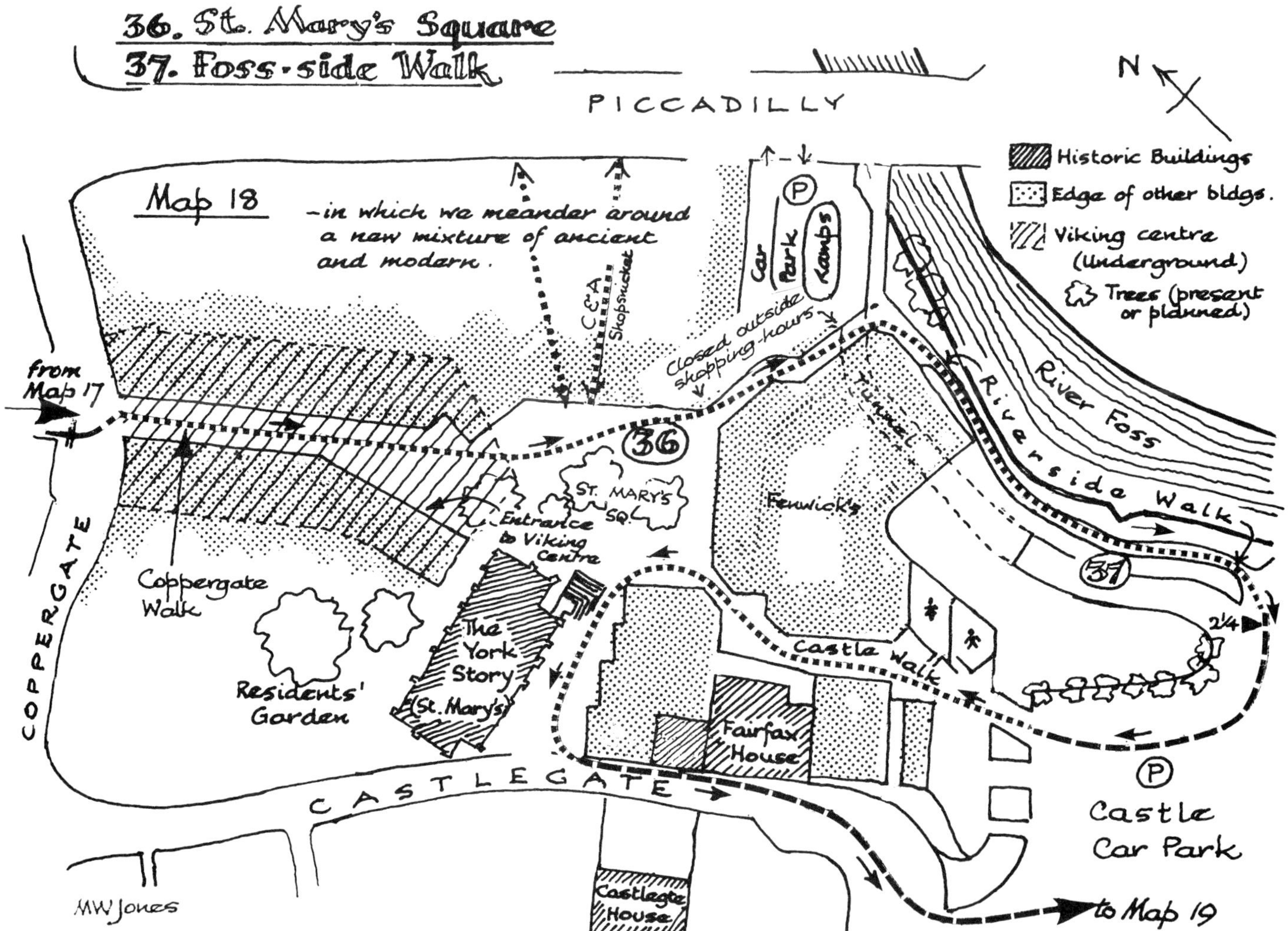
36. St. Mary's Square
37. Foss-side Walk
N
PICCADILLY
Map 18
-in which we meander around a new mixture of ancient and modern.
Historic Buildings
Edge of other bldgs.
Viking centre (Underground)
Trees (present or planned)
Car Park
P
Kamps
C&A
Shopsnicket
Closed outside shopping-hours
River Foss
Riverside Walk
Tunnel
from Map 17
36
ST. MARY'S SQ.
Entrance to Viking Centre
Fenwick's
37
2¼
Coppergate Walk
Residents' Garden
The York Story (St. Mary's)
Castle Walk
Fairfax House
COPPERGATE
CASTLEGATE
P
Castle Car Park
Castlegate House
to Map 19
MW Jones

MAP 18: St. Mary's Square

It might be argued that this new development has no place among the Snickelways. But within its bounds, it has a superb medieval church; a riverside walk beside the Foss; and above all – or rather below all – what has been described as the most exciting presentation of archeological materials in Western Europe.

Our approach will be across Coppergate (1120), the Danish for "The Street of the Woodworkers". Under the main concourse opening off Coppergate lies the excavation site, which recently yielded such important finds from the years of Viking rule in York in the 9th and 10th centuries. The entrance to the Jorvik Centre is near the northern corner of St. Mary's, in the tree-shaded St. Mary's Square.

Down a walkway to the left is the new Riverside Walk: a welcome renewal of our acquaintance with the Foss. We follow it round to the right, and when it joins the car park, concentrate on traversing in a right-hand arc: first, across the tunnel designed for cars entering this carpark from Piccadilly, then round to re-enter the precinct at Castle Walk. We come back into Central Square before turning left up past The York Story (as the exhibition housed in St. Mary's Church is called). Now that it will be surrounded by activity, this lively museum should attract the public attention that it deserves. Displaying varied aspects of every-day life as it was lived in York, it is vividly evocative of the background of our more historic Snickelways.

Castlegate, into which we now turn left out of the precinct, passes between two historic houses, both designed by John Carr, and both completed in 1762. Castlegate House, on the right, and built for the then Recorder, was grand enough. But Viscount Fairfax on the opposite side of the street went altogether more up-market. A team of hand-picked craftsmen – specialising in woodwork, stonework, metalwork and above all plasterwork – ensured that Fairfax House was to be the finest Georgian house in York. Sadly, Fairfax himself died within 10 years. After another 200 years, the house had fallen into disrepair, with hideous decor, and was described as only a "pathetic survival". But now that the York Civic Trust has proudly acquired Fairfax House, a new generation of craftsmen were set to work on the dedicated restoration of the building, so that we would be able to see it again in its real glory.

The building was duly opened by HRH the Duchess of Kent on Oct 30 1984, and was visited by 50,000 people in its first year.

So ends this Section, and another Section Map is due. But for various reasons it's postponed until p. 68

With a combination of historical accuracy, imagination, craftsmanship and technology, the Jorvik (=York) Viking Centre realistically conveys the sights, sounds and even smells of Viking every-day life.

THE JORVIK VIKING CENTRE

Long before its completion, the recreated Viking street already looked and felt part of a different age and a different world. Under utilitarian but dramatic (and sometimes eerie) lighting, the construction team were creating again the 10th Century Viking houses, pig-pens, boats and rigging, using Viking techniques to ensure authenticity. Do go and see the final, unique creation if you possibly can.

Man in a pig-pen, beside thatched, wattle-and-daub Viking house.

Rigging Viking boat

FAIRFAX HOUSE: A MUSICAL INTERLUDE

(This page was inscribed before its reopening in 1984)

2.
She
Ah! swain, was fair Belinda here
As much to her you would declare;
You men can praise each face you meet,
And still we find you all deceit:
Ne'er in your breast is love the while;
You're formed to flatter and beguile

3.
He
Believe me true, thou lovely fair,
My passion is beyond compare;
Such charms as thine make conquest sure,
And light a flame forever pure:
Whate'er thy virgin wish can crave,
'Tis but to speak, you're sure to have.

4.
She
First, as a proof you love me so,
Do you design to wed or no?
Why start you thus? 'Tis plain I see,
This is your boasted faith to me:
But, swain, I now behold the snare
I can be virtuous too and fair.

5.
He
Such sounds forever let me hear,
They're music, and they charm my ear.
She
And I am happy in my swain,
Nor envy aught around the plain;
Both
Then Hymen's sacred bands shall tie
The nuptial knot of love and joy.
(Anon)

MWJ 1984

Tantalisingly, Fairfax House continues to withhold most of its attractions, and can't yet be sketched. To tide us over until October 1984, however, we have this popular ballad of 1758, the music of which forms part of the superb plasterwork on the ceiling of the saloon. As depicted in the sketch, every note (and every sharp!) is picked out in the plaster. All I've added are the words, just unearthed for the Civic Trust from the British Library. Realism demanded that the last word of verse 1 was left out, as the plasterer hadn't room for any more music!

Fascinatingly, he precisely reproduced some of the same imperfections in the bar spacings as in the British Library's copy, suggesting that he had worked from the same printer's run-off, and that he was probably not himself a musician.

It is not known whether Belinda or Amelia had any special ties with the Fairfaxes (or the plasterer). On this evidence Belinda, dropped after the first line, had but few. The same cannot be said of the amenable Amelia.

The above craftsmanship came to light only when the ceilings were stripped of accumulations of red paint, at a cost to the Trust of £45,000

Map 19

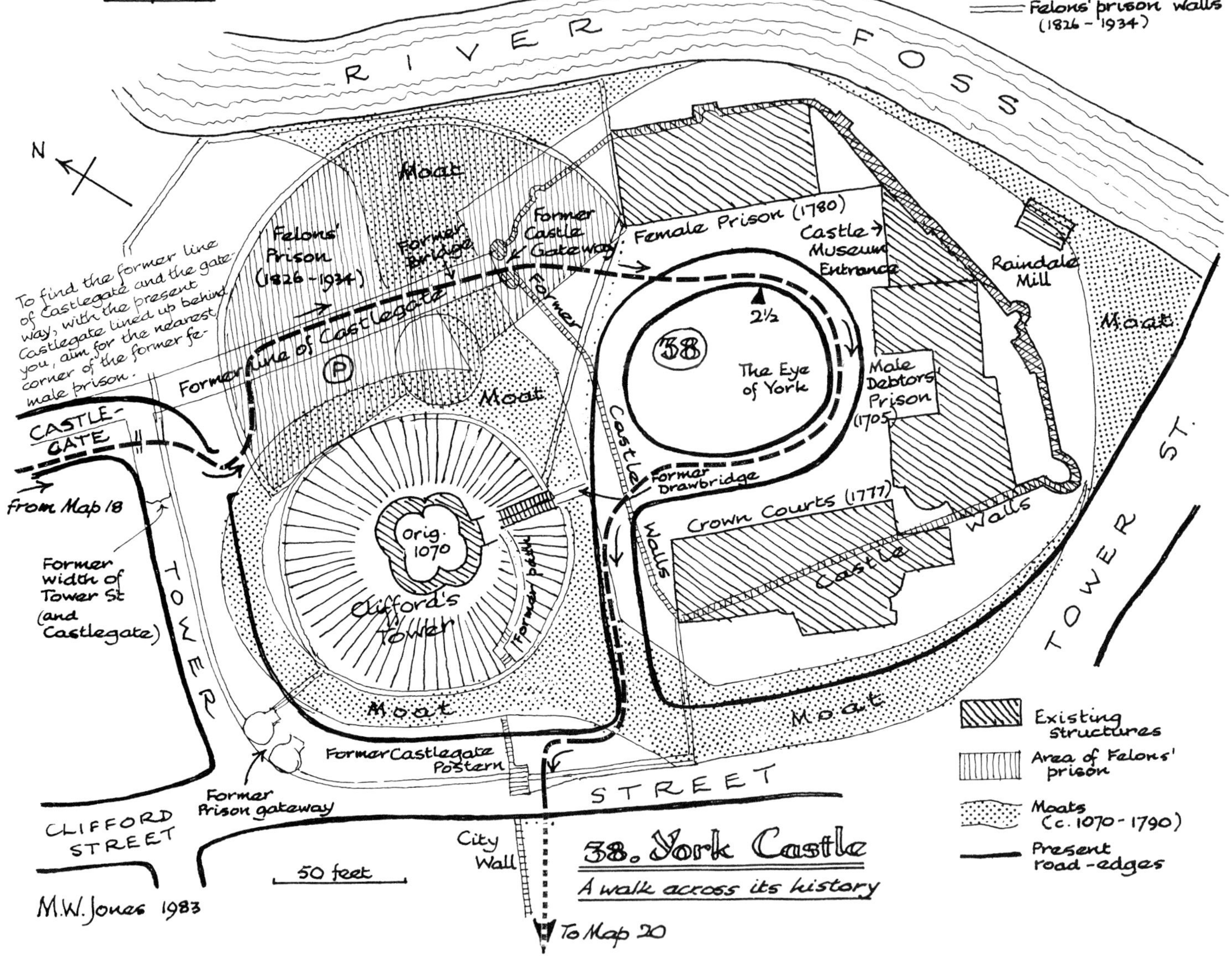
Former castle-walls
Felons' prison walls (1826 - 1934)
RIVER FOSS
N
Moat
Felons' Prison (1826-1934)
Former Bridge
Former Castle Gateway
Female Prison (1780)
Castle Museum Entrance
Raindale Mill
To find the former line of Castlegate and the gateway, with the present Castlegate lined up behind you, aim for the nearest corner of the former female prison.
Former line of Castlegate
P
Former
2½
38
The Eye of York
Male Debtors' Prison (1705)
Moat
Moat
CASTLE-GATE
From Map 18
Castle
Former Drawbridge
Crown Courts (1777)
Walls
Castle Walls
TOWER ST.
Orig. 1070
Clifford's Tower
Former path
Former width of Tower St (and Castlegate)
TOWER
Moat
Moat
Former Castlegate Postern
Former Prison gateway
STREET
CLIFFORD STREET
City Wall
50 feet
38. York Castle
A walk across its history
M.W. Jones 1983
To Map 20
Existing structures
Area of Felons' prison
Moats (c. 1070 - 1790)
Present road-edges

MAP 19: York Castle

Of all the most widely misunderstood and underestimated landmarks in York, York Castle must be the foremost. So we must now put our imagination to work, and see it not as an ocean of parked cars, but as it really was: a formidable complex for the processes of defence, administration, justice and punishment.

It developed here because this spit of land between the Rivers Foss and Ouse offered natural defences. Indeed, York itself came into existence because the Romans were so attracted by these features that they set up their legionary fortress a sixth-of-a-league from here.

But it was William the Conquerer who originated York Castle when he first arrived in 1069. Initially he built the mound and tower (originally of timber) now known as Clifford's Tower – as a foothold from which to suppress the locals. But the latter proved awkward, and he had to return not once but twice, with mounting irritation. First he built a second Mound on the other side of the Ouse (Baile Hill) and then developed the castle proper.

Most people think that Clifford's tower is York Castle; but it's only a part of it. The Castle Walls – high, extensive and imperious – surrounded most of the area before us. Surrounding them in turn was a Moat, fed from the River Foss, the level of which had therefore to be raised by damming it just below the Castle. (It remained thus until The Foss was made navigable in 1794). Another Moat extended round the base of the mound (or MOTTE). Castlegate, instead of taking its evasive corner to the right, ran straight on across the Moat, into the Castle. Also within the walls were the Bailey, or general parade ground, and administrative buildings from which York was ruled. The defences were completed by the replacement of the wooden tower with the present stone structure in about 1250 – some time after the appalling suicide in the tower, under mob pressure, of some 150 Jews.

Not until the 18th Century were the Male Debtors' and Female Prisons built, along with the Assize Courts. Though no consolation to their hapless inmates, the thought strikes one that few prisons can have looked less oppressive – externally – than these. But we must remember that they were still surrounded by the great and formidable outer walls. Of less attractive appearance was the subsequent Felons' Prison (that is, for criminals), built in 1826 after the draining of the Moat. Surrounded by its own huge wall, it sat right across the castle approach – i.e. in the middle of the car-park – until its removal in 1934.

I've attempted opposite to show, from various (sometimes conflicting) old maps, roughly where everything was. The old street over the Moat and into the Castle was in line with Castlegate. As we now pick our way through the cars and round the Eye of York, we spare a thought for all (mostly poor and unsung) who went before us across this page of history....

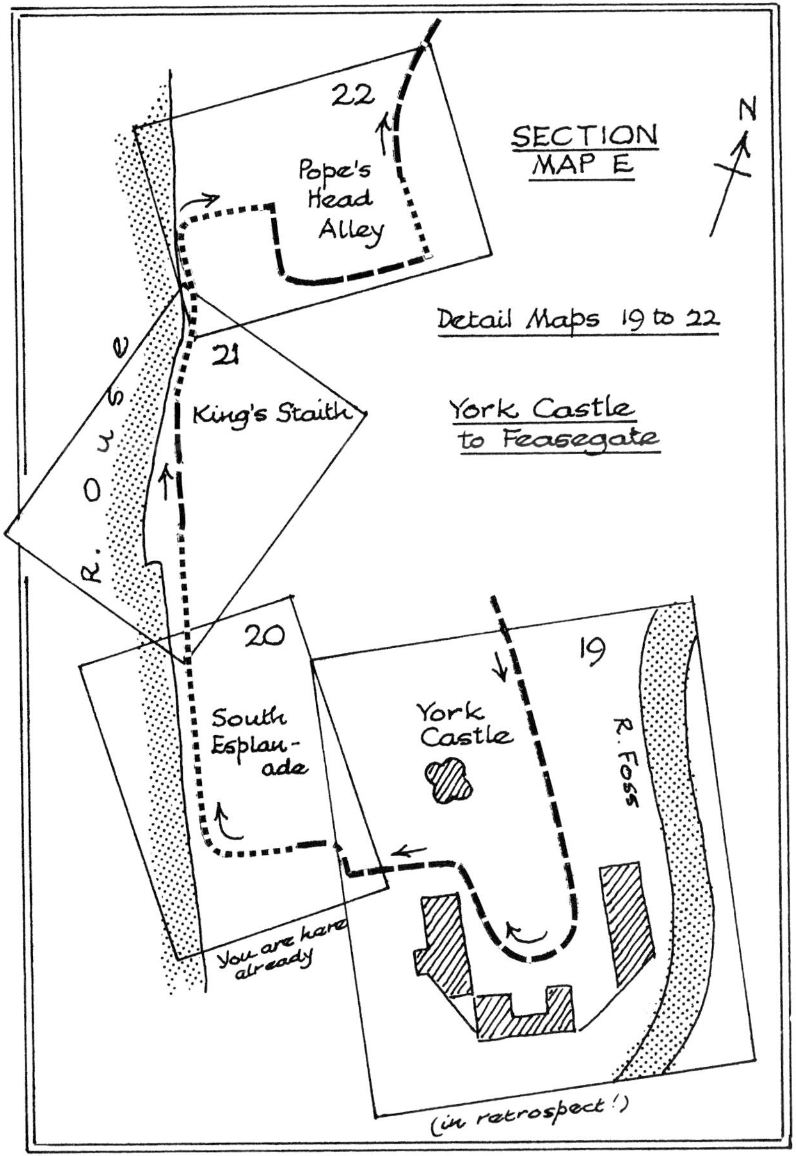
SECTION MAP E
Detail Maps 19 to 22
York Castle to Feasegate
N
22
Pope's Head Alley
21
King's Staith
R. Ouse
20
South Esplanade
You are here already
19
York Castle
R. Foss
(in retrospect!)

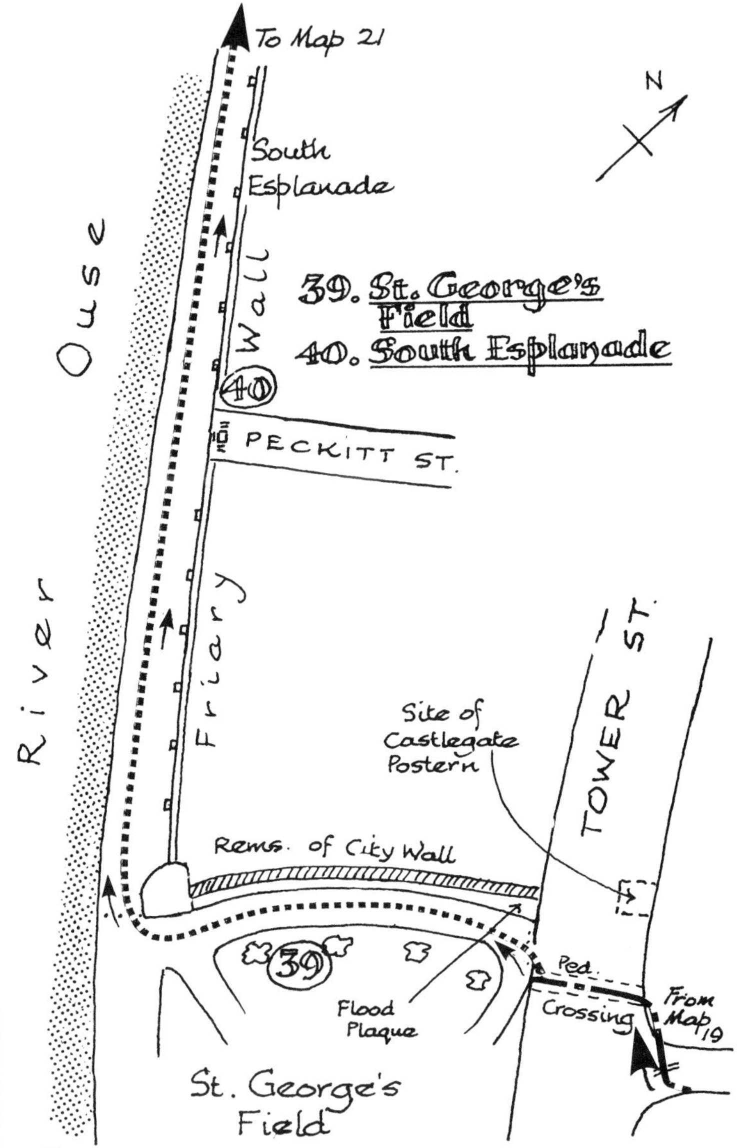
To Map 21
N
South Esplanade
39. St. George's Field
40. South Esplanade
River Ouse
Friary Wall
40
PECKITT ST.
TOWER ST.
Site of Castlegate Postern
Rems. of City Wall
39
Flood Plaque
Ped. Crossing
From Map 19
St. George's Field

Map 20

MAP 20: St. George's Field - Friars' Walk

A pedestrian-crossing now conveniently takes us across Tower-Street, almost along the line of where the City Wall linked the Castle Walls to the River Ouse. But the river itself, apart from being a defence, was also an invader.

Strictly, the Ouse starts less than 20 miles above York, at a point near the confluence of two of its tributaries, the Swale and the Ure. But the headwaters of these two rivers are ninety river-miles away, near the north-western edge of the high, rainswept Pennines. Indeed, they both rise within a couple of miles of the feeders of the River Eden, which flows out to the Solway Firth; so that there is an almost unbroken watercourse between York and south-west Scotland. It is these great, high catchment areas that periodically send their floods down to York. The worst over the last 3½ centuries are recorded on a plaque on the city wall, just through the gate into Saint George's Field. Surprisingly, the 16'7" flood of 1982 hasn't yet been added.* I've anticipated it in the sketch.

St. George's Field extends as far as the confluence with the Foss, 500 yards downstream, but it was divided when Skeldergate Bridge was built in 1881. The northern part remains an attractive little public park. Its attractions must however have been lost upon the FLYTERS, defined as female scolds, who were subjected to the ducking-stool nearby; and even moreso upon the victims hanged on the gallows on this side of the Law Courts. Huge crowds used to gather here to watch: As recently as 1862, people came specially by excursion train.

Leaving behind us these scenes of retribution, we turn right at the end of the City Wall, along the pleasant South Esplanade beside the river and an old Friary wall.

* Now updated! (1999)

Flood-levels: St. George's Field
(These heights are over and above normal river-level)

MAP 21: King's Staith

Even the peaceful footpath along South Esplanade, beside the old Friary wall, runs close to the scene of ancient controversy. A Franciscan Friary, founded by Henry II, extended right up to Castlegate, and from Friargate to St. George's Field. Royalty was entertained here at intervals. But after three centuries, a row broke out between Henry VIII and the Franciscans, who tried to thwart his second marriage, to Anne Boleyn. The result: his confiscation of the Friary in 1538.

The river attracts our attention again. Today it's used mostly by pleasure-boats. But historically, it was of critical importance to travellers – particularly to invaders. Until comparatively recently, water transport was the best way of shifting large quantities of anything, including invading armies. As we've seen, the Romans used the Ouse (then tidal to York) to penetrate deep into northern England to establish Eboracum. Then, in 867, the Vikings mounted a massive landing operation, with up to 350 longboats sweeping up the Ouse on the high tide to put their warriors ashore on this very riverbank.

Thereafter it was the Ouse that provided the route for York's trading for centuries to come. The greatest concentration of activity was at King's Staith. In the 17th Century Queen's Staith, on the opposite bank, was built, and subsequently developed as the main landing for bulk cargoes including coal, butter and cocoa-beans. By this time Naburn lock had been built in 1757, and the river at York was non-tidal. Fifty years later, regular steam-packet passenger boats started an 8-hour service between Skeldergate wharf and Hull, which continued until 1870.

We now skirt the low wall and railings on our right, and thread our way through the quayside car-park, where drivers risk returning to find their cars

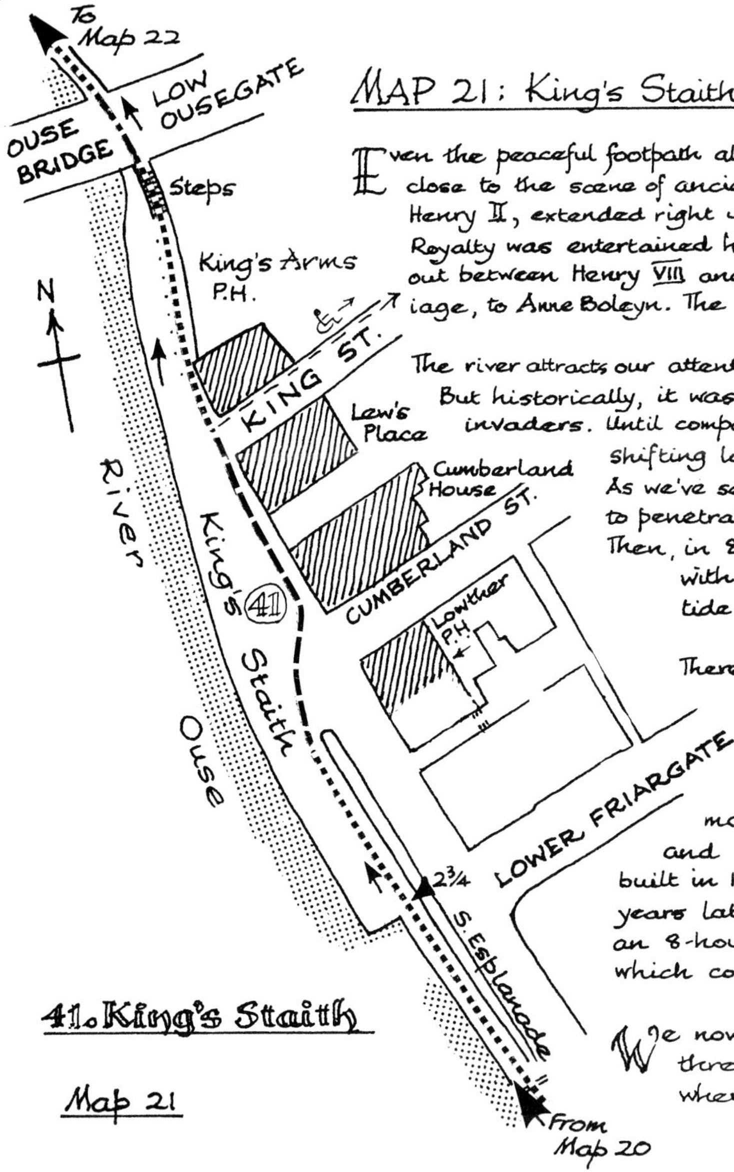

41. King's Staith

Map 21

King's Staith

Sitting one evening outside the King's Arms, our charming Dutch guest suddenly asked:
"What does zis mean – 'Use ze 'ouse'?"
"Use the house?" we asked, puzzled.
"Yes – Look!", she said, pointing over the river at the large slogan on the wall of the warehouse opposite:
"USE THE OUSE"*
Then the penny dropped! But she wasn't the first, I later found, to pronounce Ouse as a good Yorkshireman would pronounce House. In 1685 a mapmaker named Rickards (a Welshman?) carefully spelt it as the RIVER OWSE, thus leaving no room for doubt.
So the rest of us must have got it all wrong.

inundated by the rapidly-rising Ouse† (Not so the York Magistrates, whose reserved parking is usually above flood level, and-quite-right-too.) On our right is the handsome Georgian Cumberland House, built in 1700 for Alderman William Cornwell. The house must have been hemmed-in by squalor; for this street was formerly one of the notorious Water Lanes that ran down from Castlegate to the Staith, which in 1858 were said to contain "nothing but dens of infamy". King Street was another.

† Since 1996, we have been prohibited from taking this risk

Both streets, rebuilt by 1881 (when Clifford Street was created) now provide strategic corners where they join King's Staith for a succession of good hostelries – the Lowther, Law's Place and the King's Arms. Relaxing at a table outside the latter on a warm summer's evening, under a sunshade and with suitable refreshment, you can contentedly imagine that you're somewhere on the continent. And you can forget that in flood-time (as shown on the flood-gauge on the nearby arch of Ouse Bridge) your head would be under three feet of water!

* This slogan, alas, was removed in 1983

MAP 22: Ouse Bridge – Feasegate

We now ascend the steps (formerly curiously called SALTHOLE GRESE) onto Ouse Bridge. Leaning on its eminent and comfortable parapet, it's interesting to reflect that for some 1,000 years the only bridge over the Ouse was at this point. Moreover, for most of that time there was no other bridge between York and the North Sea. So it was a crossing of extraordinary importance not just for York but for the whole north-east corner of the kingdom, and carried the main road from London to the North.

Not of course that this one is the original bridge. The first, a wooden structure, was probably put up about 850 A.D. But in 1154 a throng of admirers stood on it to welcome Archbishop William (later Saint William, of the College – see p 40) and the lot, apart from William, collapsed into the river. It was replaced by a five-arched stone structure, steep and narrow, which like the Foss Bridge (p.55) was crammed with buildings. They included a chapel, a hospital and a prison – a sort of medieval service-station.

In 1564, hardly surprising after some 350 years of wear-and-tear, the two central arches were battered down by flood and ice, and the bridge was rebuilt with a single central arch to replace the two. Finally, the present bridge was erected, by

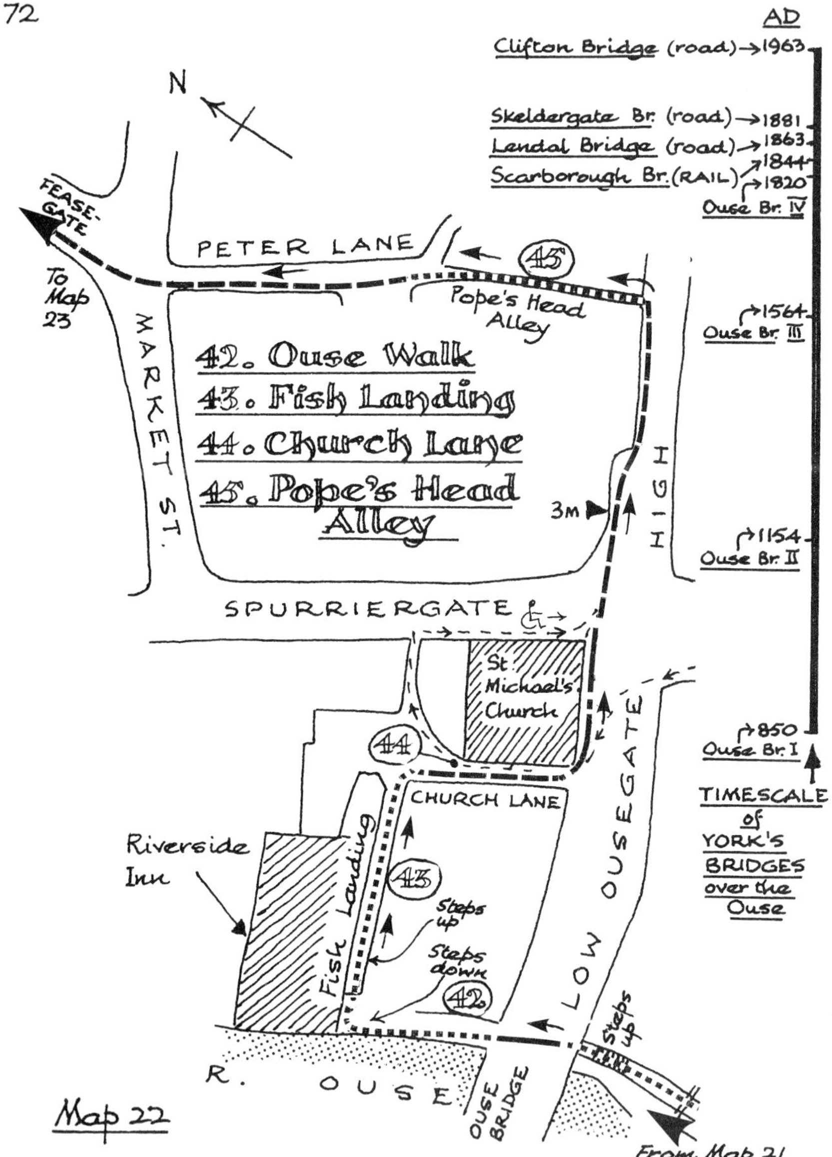

Map 22

plan this time and not disaster, in 1820. But during all this period no alternative crossing had been built, and indeed the first such was not a road bridge but the Scarboro' railway bridge. The time-scale shows how Ouse Bridge stood alone through most of York's history.

At last we move on, carefully crossing the road with its heavy modern traffic, to the short and newish Ouse Walk (nameless, so we give it our own title). This leads us to a rather disagreeable downward flight of steps, which seems to be getting us nowhere. But provided that there are no floods around, we find ourselves in a more authentic Snickelway: the old Fish Landing, a medieval Common Lane, along which the fish was carted from river to market.

Instinct would now take us straight on through the archway; but instead, on reaching an attractive courtyard, we turn right down another Common Lane, Church Lane, so-called because it served the 12th-century St. Michael's Church. Confronted again by the busy Low Ousegate, we turn left (trying at the same time to note the ornamental clock above us) and pick our way across Spurriergate (Spurmakers' Street) into High Ousegate.

The next Snickelway entry is the easiest of all to miss. It lurks to the left, in a gap between two shop-front pillars, and takes us into a dark and narrow chasm evocative of an earlier experience. For this is Pope's Head Alley (so Drake informs us) and is the companion to Le Kyrk Lane, of our erstwhile acquaintance. And so out into Peter Lane and the light of day, keeping of course to the left. Somehow, it feels less oppressive now than on our first encounter!

Church Lane MWJ

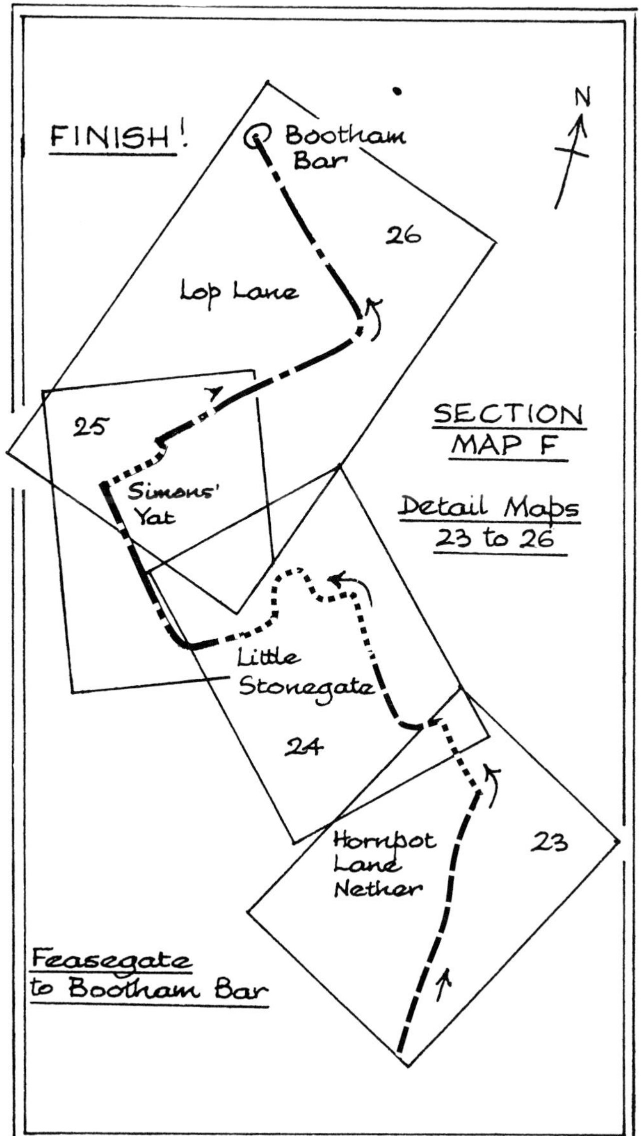
FINISH!
Bootham Bar
N
26
Lop Lane
25
SECTION MAP F
Simons' Yat
Detail Maps 23 to 26
Little Stonegate
24
Hornpot Lane Nether
23
Feasegate to Bootham Bar

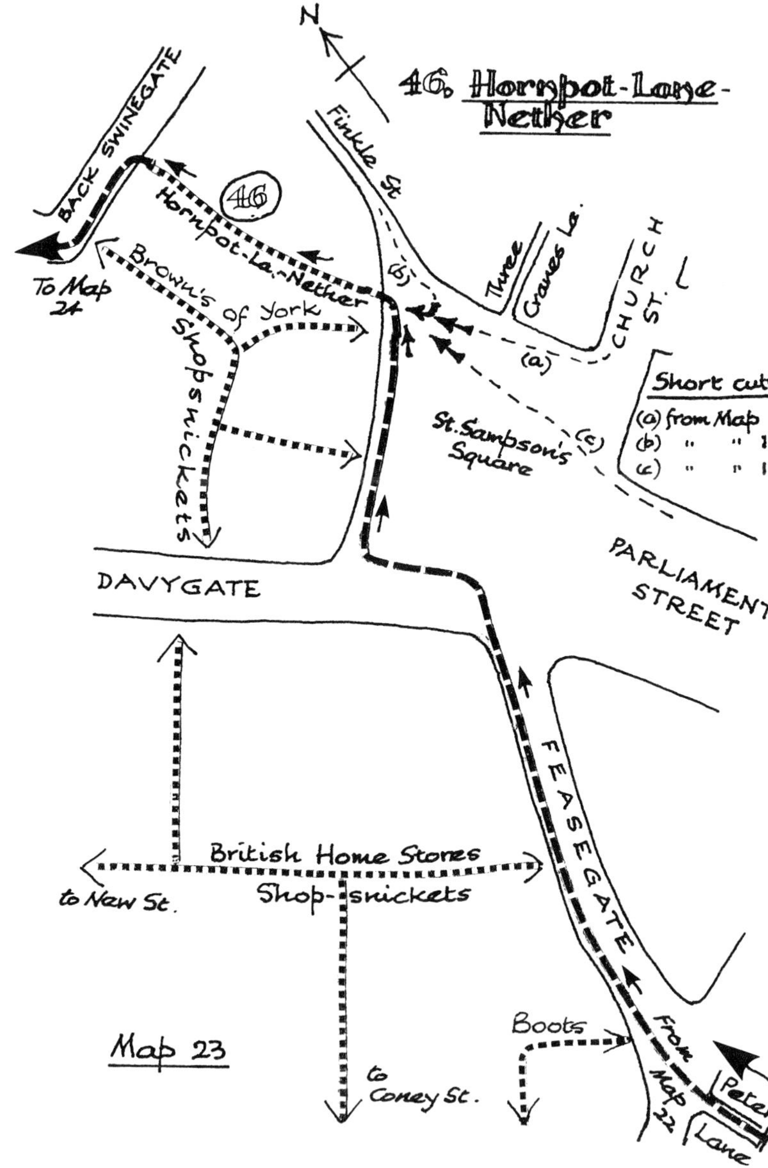
N
46. Hornpot-Lane-Nether
BACK SWINEGATE
Finkle St
46
Hornpot-La.-Nether
To Map 24
Brown's of York
Shopsnickets
Three Cranes La.
CHURCH ST.
(b)
(a)
Short cuts
(a) from Map 6
(b) " " 12
(c) " " 17
St. Sampson's Square
(c)
DAVYGATE
PARLIAMENT STREET
FEASEGATE
British Home Stores
to New St.
Shop-snickets
Boots
Map 23
to Coney St.
From Map 22
Peter Lane

MAP 23: Feasegate–Hornpot-Lane-Nether

Though short of Snickelways – it has only one – this page has a double claim to importance.

First, it has the biggest cluster of Shopsnickets: Brown's of York, British Home Stores and Boots the Chemist, offer a variety of useful means of getting from one place to another (see p. 85)

Second, it's the gathering-ground of the short-cutters, who left our route earlier, and now converge with us in triumphal procession on Hornpot-Lane-Nether, the Clapham Junction of the S-ways.

To reach it, those of us who have survived the full course must first make our way up Feasegate – formerly Fehus or Cowhouse Street (1259) – and into the Thursday Market, which we encounter for the third and last time. In the 15th Century, we would have found here a market cross. If only we still had one, as a focal point for the Square's activities...

Hornpot-Lane-Nether leads off to the left at the entrance to Finkle Street. It is our last real ginnel, and we savour its three tunnels, its uncompromising walls of curving brick, and its narrow decadence. As for its name, Jeffries in 1773 marked it as Hornpot Lane, so we simply add the Nether (old English NIOTHERA, or "further down") to distinguish it from its Holy Trinity namesake.

Hornpot-Lane-Nether MWJ

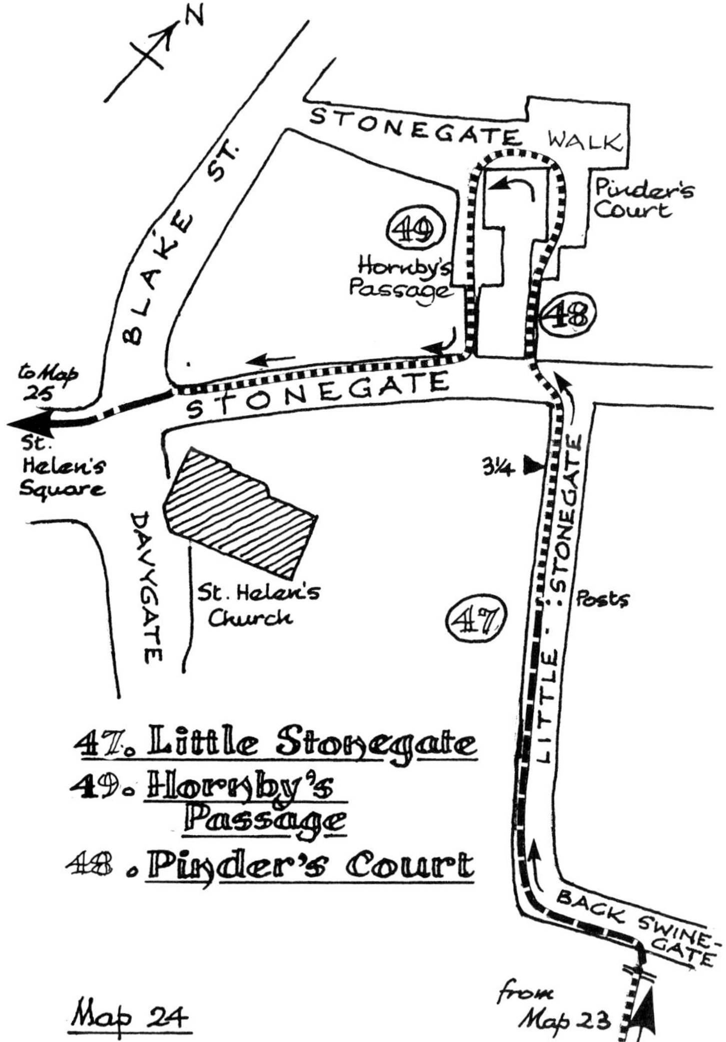

Map 24

1983

MAP 24 Back Swinegate/Blake St.

Where once pigs ran squealing on their way to the Swinegate market, now only people (and not very many of them) make their way between the posts that guard the northern end of Little Stonegate. We re-enter Stonegate under the gaze of a seafaring lady of unusual figure (more attractive in profile than frontally) who impels us across the street to the entrance to Pinder's Court.

Not that you would see that name here: the sign says Stonegate Walk. But this is only the collective name for a new collection of Snickelways, a creation that excitingly and satisfyingly blends old and new. Walk up the passage into a little courtyard, and you unexpectedly see the Minster, framed by a spacious glazed canopy. Look back, and you are greeted by a back-door view of Stonegate and its roofs – the deliciously random yet harmonious pattern of medieval buildings, with which we've become familiar in our nearly-completed wanderings. For Pinder's Court, and its parallel companion, Hornby's Passage, which are at the heart of the Stonegate Walk, form a happy and fitting penultimate to our list of fifty Snickelways. In their case, the surprise is that not so many years ago, this attractive area was the dank, dark, oily and echoing City Garage. How many more ancient Snickelways lie behind York's shop-fronts and warehouses, awaiting rediscovery and re-birth?

Completing our visit through Hornby's Passage, we come back into Stonegate, turn right past the 17th Century Punch Bowl Inn, and continue on into St. Helen's Square.

Little Stonegate

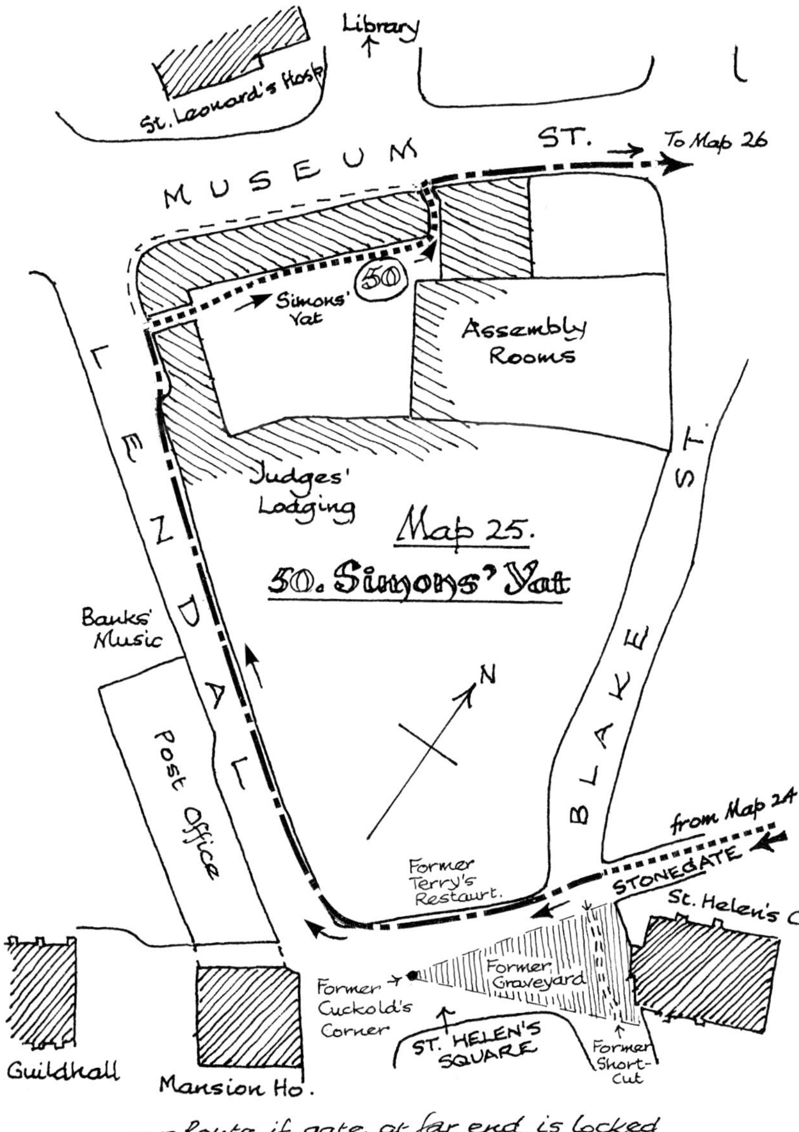

MAP 25 (St Helen's Sq. – Museum St.)

Some have said that since the sad closure in 1980 of Terry's restaurant, and the removal thereby of discernible human activity, St Helen's Square has become a graveyard. If that is so (with apologies to Betty's, which still thrives on the opposite side) then history is only repeating itself.

For until the 18th Century, most of the Square was literally the graveyard of St. Helen's Church. In the shape of a triangle, it jutted southwestwards, forming a tiresome obstacle for people on their way from Blake Street into Davygate. But human nature ensured that a track was beaten through the graveyard, by-passing the corner of the triangle. This corner was known for some reason as Cuckold's Corner. Was it because, while husbands stood there unsuspectingly admiring the grandeur of the Mansion House, their wives took the short-cut behind their backs? If so, these irregularities were put a stop to in 1745, when the graveyard was removed to a plot further down Davygate.

The Mansion House, completed in 1732, is unique. Quite apart from its outstanding elegance, it pre-dates London's Mansion House. Moreover, it is the only formal residence for a Lord Mayor in the country in which he or she actually resides seven days a week.

The passage through the archway to the right

was formerly the continuation of Stonegate, and led down to the river. It still does, but only as a narrow subterranean passage, the medieval Common Hall Lane, which passes under the Guildhall to a former jetty. Unfortunately it isn't normally available to the public.

We turn right therefore past the Post Office (surprisingly on this site for 270 years) into Lendal, whose name derives from St. Leonard's Lending (landing) Hill. Until the 16th century the area to left was the site of yet another friary. On the right is the Judges' Lodging, built around 1720 but not actually lodging judges until 1800.

Just before the end of Lendal, on the right, we come to our last (and York's latest) Snickelway. It leads us under a high archway framing the Minster, and through an attractively-designed and paved service-yard – compare it with the eyesore in Cheat's Lane (p. 58) which serves a similar purpose! In the far left-hand corner, where once was the most tasteful dustbin-shelter you've ever seen, is an authentic little passageway with flagstones, cobbles and a bend – an imaginative touch reminiscent of some earlier Snickelways.

This Snickelway lacked a name, so again we had to invent one. The old yards were often named after their builders. This was built by SIMONS. And the old English for gate or gap is YAT. Hence Simons' Yat. So at a stroke, York now has an answer to its namesake by the River Wye – albeit more workaday, and spelt in a less highfalutin way than the Symonds down at the other yat.

We emerge from our yat into Museum Street, opposite the remains of St. Leonard's Hospital, and the less ancient Central Library – in whose rich reference section one's reading is accompanied by the calls of peacocks in the Museum Gardens close by.

Simons' Yat

1999: The gate at the far end may now, alas, be locked....

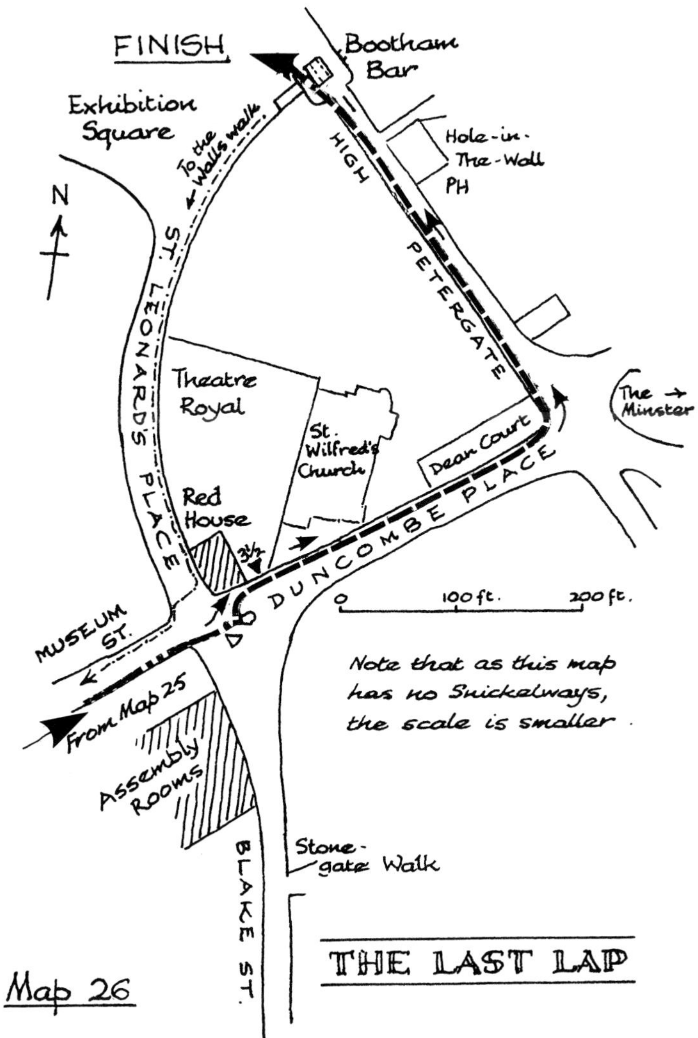

Map 26

Map 25 Blake Street – Bootham Bar

With all 50 Snickelways now behind us, all that remains is to stroll – with a modest sense of accomplishment – back to our starting-point. Appropriately, this last two hundred yards arranges itself into a reverse playback of the time-span that we've encountered.

On the right we see the comparatively-recent Assembly Rooms. They were built in 1732, to the design of the Earl of Burlington, as a place where the local and visiting gentry could amuse themselves in the evening after a hard day's work at the races or the Assize Courts. With music, dancing, cards, dice and drinking (if only tea) they must have been a distinctly high-class 18th-Century night-club.

We cross Duncombe Place at the traffic-lights, with the Red House facing us. It's clearly a corner house. But it found itself on a corner only after 120 years, when in 1834 St Leonard's Place was cut through. We leave the latter alone (for later use by those who wish to walk the Walls) and instead turn right down what used to be the narrow Lop Lane (page 41)

Before us once again rises the Minster. Humbly we reflect that this great and glorious building has towered above the streets and Snickelways of York for over 500 years, that it was there before most of them, and that its construction was the work of ten generations. If we had the faith and conviction of those who laid its foundations, we would now be turning to our picks and shovels, to make a start on a building to be completed in about AD 2,230.

Instead of which we move yet further back in time, along High Petergate and back to Bootham Bar: to the ancient gateway first established by the Romans, and the start of it all.

And for us, the finish.

"In Petergate I end my general ſurvey of the city and ſuburbs, a long and tedious march. I am ſenſible how dull and tireſome it must be for the reader to follow me quite through this peregrination; but he muſt therefore reflect what a taſk it has been to the firſt wanderer to find his way in ſuch a labyrinth of imperfect mazes and obſcurities."

— *Francis Drake, 1736*

THE END

Bootham Bar

SOME OPTIONAL EXTRAS

(A) THE GREATEST SNICKELWAY (The Walls)

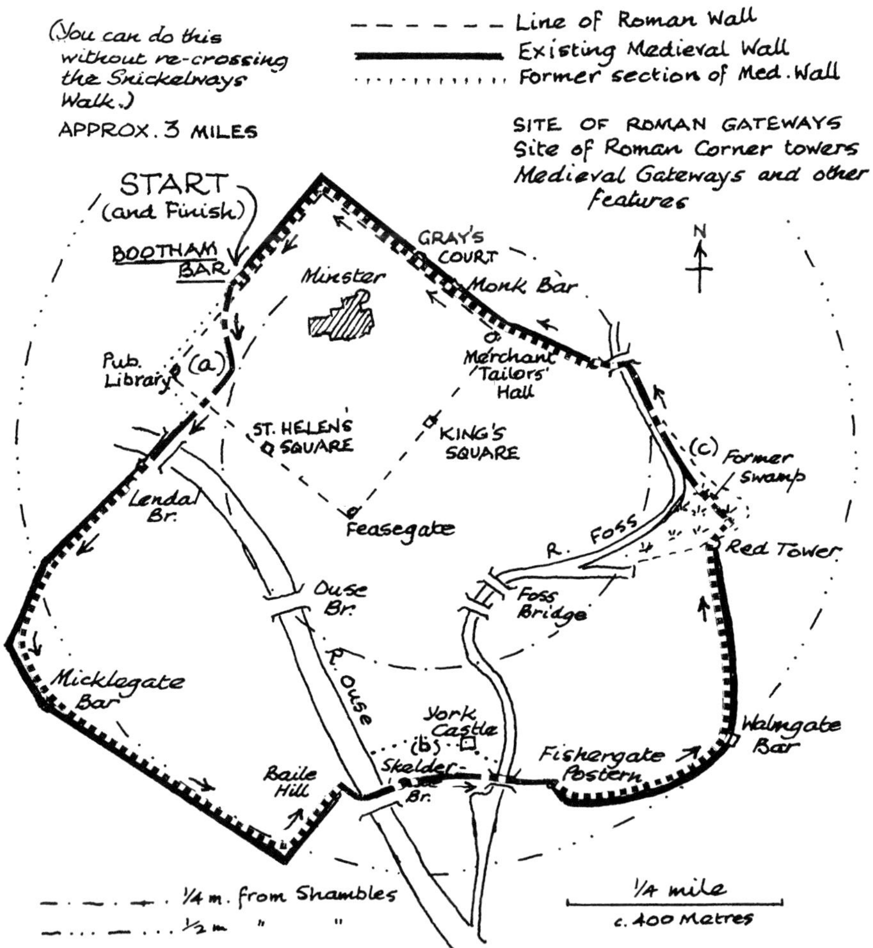

The Walls are such impressive fortifications that it's surprising to find three large gaps in their continuity. But these are all easily explained:

(a) Bootham Bar to Lendal Bridge

The Walls used to march straight on into Museum Gardens, then left at the multangular tower and right near the library, to form an uninterrupted line to the River Ouse. But this link was broken in 1834 with the building of St. Leonard's Place, along which we are now diverted towards Lendal Bridge.

(b) Baile Hill to Fishergate Postern

With the Baile Hill mound guarding the west bank of the Ouse, the wall was immediately resumed on the opposite bank, and linked up at Castlegate Postern with the walls of York Castle itself. The Castle in turn abutted onto the Foss, on the opposite bank of which the wall resumed (as it still does) at Fishergate Postern.

(c) Red Tower to Layerthorpe Bridge

This gap was plugged by an area of swampy land, flooded by the damming of the Foss below the castle. (The latter also served to fill the moats surrounding the Castle and Clifford's Tower – see page 44).

Optional Extras (Continued)

Carr's Lane — MWJ

(B) THE WEST BANK SNICKELWAYS

Another seven for your bag. They can be linked in with the main Snickelways walk at Ouse Bridge, or added as an afterthought. Much street-walking (by you, I mean) but mostly fairly traffic-free.

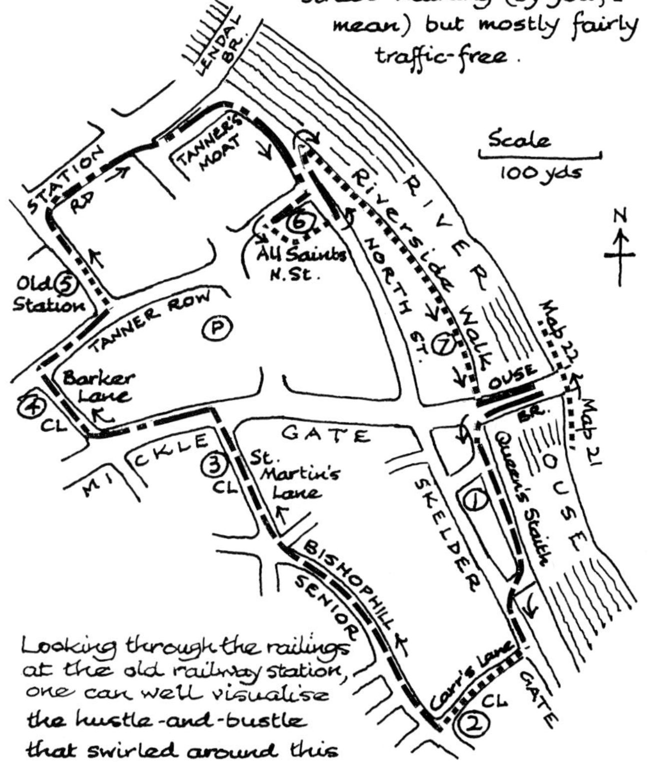

Looking through the railings at the old railway station, one can well visualise the hustle-and-bustle that swirled around this beautiful piece of railway architecture in its hey-day in the 1840s to 60s.

CL = Medieval Common Lane

Optional Extras (Continued)

Ⓒ YORK'S LONGEST SNICKET

(About 1 mile)

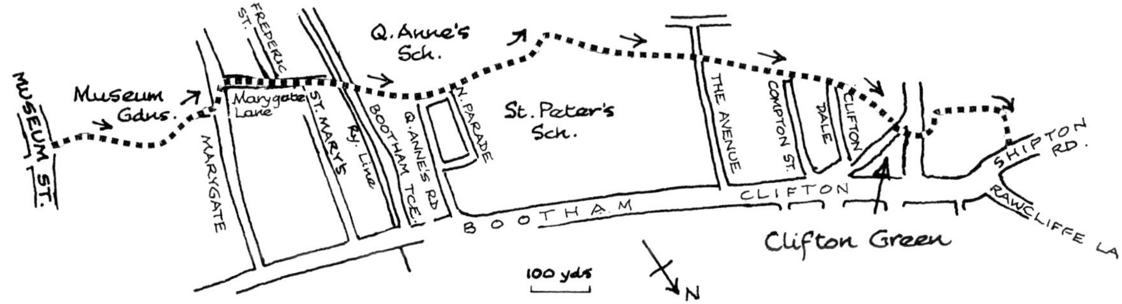

Ⓓ YORK'S OLDEST and LONGEST GINNEL

(½ mile)

The old Roman route from the forest of Galtres to the Eboracum fortress

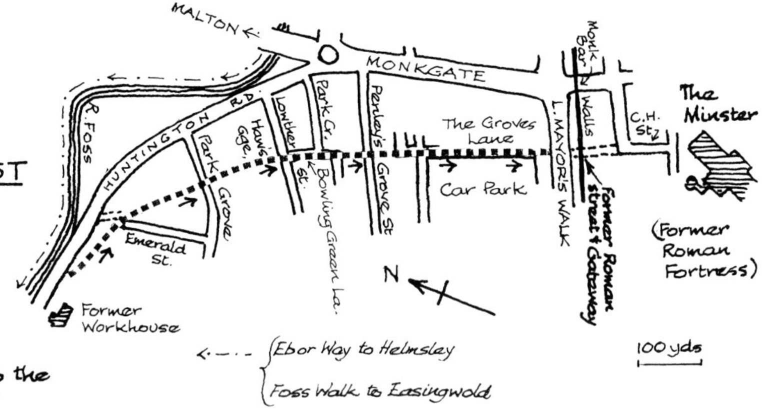

OPTIONAL EXTRA (E): A Foul-Weather Snickelroute: Bootham Bar to Castle Museum

A route for the connoisseur of Snickelways and Shopsnickets. (For this purpose, the Minster comes under Shopsnicket Rules: you should enter as a normal and respectful attender, have an interest in its affairs, and possess the means to make a contribution.)

The route is but one of countless permutations. Try your own – e.g. from the Assembly Rooms to the Foss

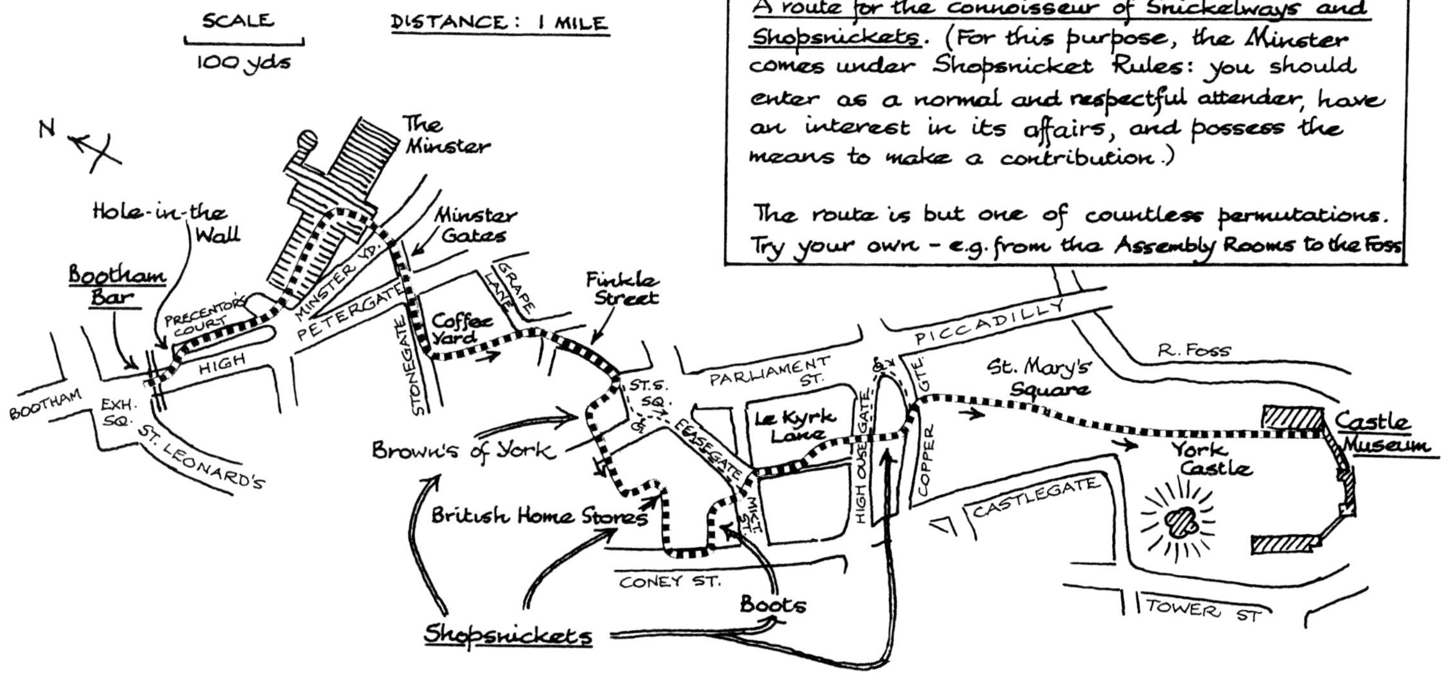

Along the way, you could be tempted by a wide range of Shopsnicket wares: a sink-plunger, butter-muslin or a bed (W.P. Brown); an electric spotlight, a gorgonzola or a pair of trousers (B.H.S); milk of magnesia, an alarm clock or eyeshadow (Boots); a putty-knife, coving or a stripper.

Thus encumbered, you must nevertheless hope to buy, in the Coppergate Precinct, an umbrella, as the last 150 yards, across to the Castle Museum, offers no shelter. Not, at least, until they excavate and display the cellars of the former felons' prison; but for this, we shall have to wait until about 3000 AD.

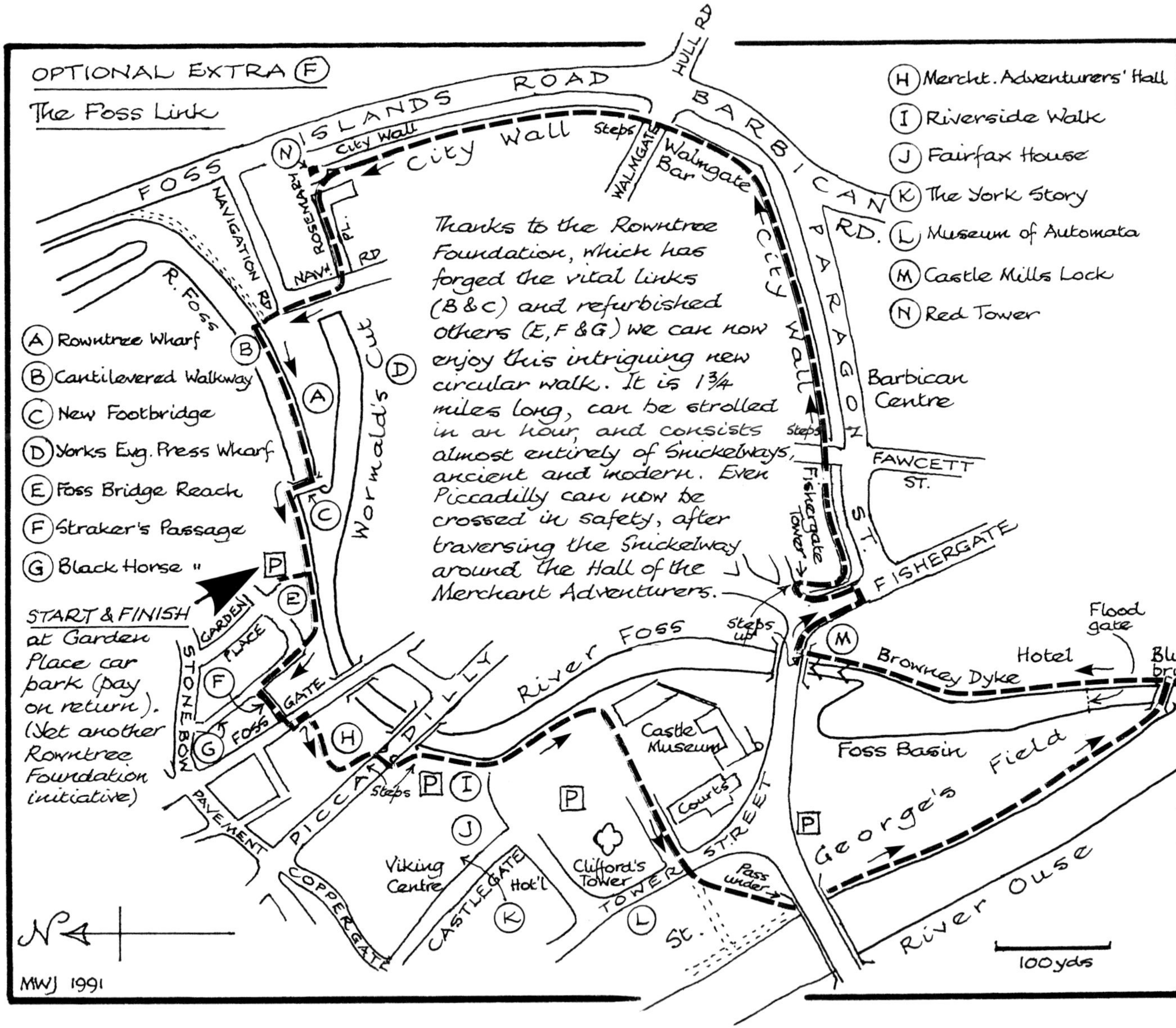
OPTIONAL EXTRA (F)
The Foss Link
(H) Mercht. Adventurers' Hall
(I) Riverside Walk
(J) Fairfax House
(K) The York Story
(L) Museum of Automata
(M) Castle Mills Lock
(N) Red Tower
(A) Rowntree Wharf
(B) Cantilevered Walkway
(C) New Footbridge
(D) Yorks Evg. Press Wharf
(E) Foss Bridge Reach
(F) Straker's Passage
(G) Black Horse "
START & FINISH at Garden Place car park (pay on return). (Yet another Rowntree Foundation initiative)
Thanks to the Rowntree Foundation, which has forged the vital links (B&C) and refurbished others (E, F & G) we can now enjoy this intriguing new circular walk. It is 1¾ miles long, can be strolled in an hour, and consists almost entirely of Snickelways, ancient and modern. Even Piccadilly can now be crossed in safety, after traversing the Snickelway around the Hall of the Merchant Adventurers.
FOSS ISLANDS ROAD
HULL RD
BARBICAN RD.
City Wall
City Wall
Steps
WALMGATE
Walmgate Bar
City Wall
PARAGON ST.
Barbican Centre
Steps
FAWCETT ST.
FISHERGATE
Fishergate Tower
Steps up
NAVIGATION RD
ROSEMARY PL.
NAVN. RD
R. Foss
Wormald's Cut
GARDEN PLACE
STONEBOW
FOSS GATE
PAVEMENT
PICCADILLY
Steps
River Foss
Castle Museum
Courts
Clifford's Tower
Viking Centre
CASTLEGATE
Hot'l
COPPERGATE
TOWER ST.
Pass under
Browney Dyke
Hotel
Flood gate
Blue bridge
Foss Basin
George's Field
River Ouse
100yds
MWJ 1991

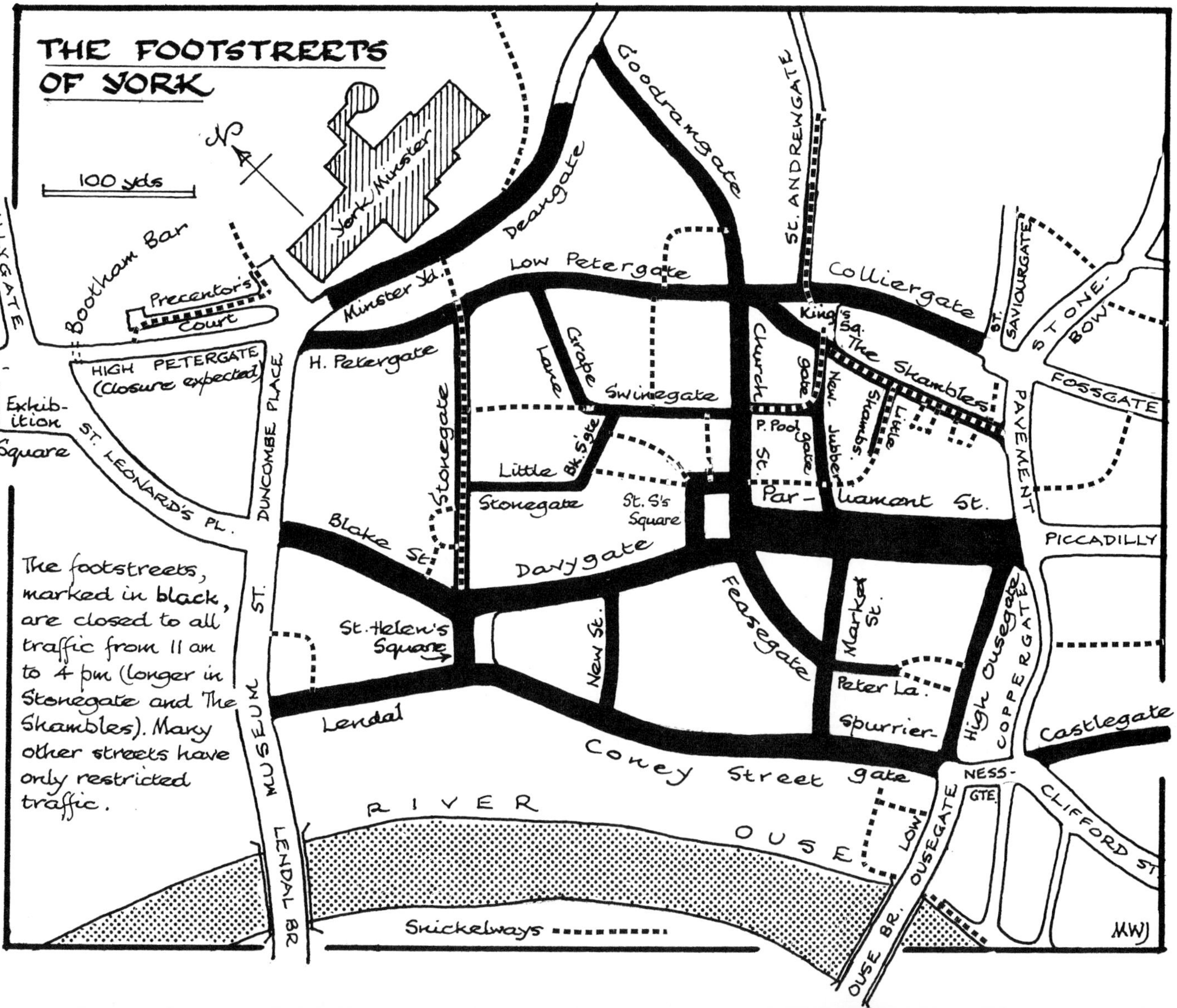
THE FOOTSTREETS OF YORK
N
100 yds
York Minster
Goodramgate
St. Andrewgate
Deangate
Bootham Bar
Precentor's Court
Minster Yd.
Low Petergate
Colliergate
St. Saviourgate
Stonebow
Gillygate
Bootham
Exhibition Square
High Petergate (Closure expected)
H. Petergate
St. Leonard's Pl.
Duncombe Place
Stonegate
Grape Lane
Swinegate
Church St.
King's Sq.
Gate
The Shambles
New Jubbergate
Little Shambles
P. Pool gate
Fossgate
Pavement
Little Bk. S'gte
Little Stonegate
St. S's Square
Parliament St.
Piccadilly
Blake St.
Davygate
Feasegate
Market St.
St. Helen's Square
New St.
High Ousegate
Coppergate
Peter La.
Spurrier-gate
Castlegate
St. Museum St.
Lendal
Coney Street
Ness-gte.
Clifford St
River Ouse
Low Ousegate
Ouse Br.
Lendal Br.
Snickelways
MWJ
The footstreets, marked in black, are closed to all traffic from 11 am to 4 pm (longer in Stonegate and The Shambles). Many other streets have only restricted traffic.

A-WHEEL THROUGH THE SNICKELWAYS ←

Nearly all of the Snickelways Walk is "go-able" for an accompanied wheelchairist – even the narrow chasms of Le Kyrk Lane and Pope's Head Alley. Where the occasional obstructions do arise, there's always an alternative, marked on the map thus: ♿ - → - - . Altogether you can pass unobstructed through 43 out of the 50 Snickelways.

Map	Page	HAZARD	RECOMMENDED COURSE
4	25	Penny Lane now obstructed by posts	Proceed along St. Andrewgate
13	48	Snickelways 24 and 25 obstructed by posts	Enter Market from Shambles through S-way 23, omit 24 and 25, then exit through No. 26.
" 14	49 52	Snickelway 27 obstructed by post. Lower Stonebow hostile to all crossers especially wheelchairists.	Go round far side of St. Crux Parish Room, then cross Whipmawhopmagate and Stonebow at traffic islands. Go down S. side of Stonebow, Black Horse Passage
15	54	Steps up from Foss Bridge Reach	Have a look at Foss Bridge Reach, go back up Garden Place, go left then right and head for Straker's Passage.
16	58	Steps up in Lady Peckett's Yard	Continue up Fossgate, turn left along Pavement
21 22	70 72	Steps up to Ouse Bridge Steps down to Fish Landing, then up	Divert R. up King St. (a bit steep), L. into Nessgate, L. again down far side of Low Ousegate. Turn R. into Church Lane, then R. again up Upper Fish Landing (which the others missed) through archway into Spurriergate, then R. to High Ousegate, to join the homeward trail.

CLASSIFICATION OF THE SNICKELWAYS

Arc = Arcade
Ch = Churchyard
CL = Medieval Common Lane
G = Ginnel
M = Medieval Street
P = Passage(way)
Pr = Precinct
Pw = Open Pathway
R = Roofed, wholly or partly
Rv = Riverside Pathway
Y = Yard, Court or Courtyard
S = Snicket

NO.	MAP		TYPE	MIN.* WIDTH
1	1	Hole-in-the-Wall	CL,P,R	2'11"
2	2	Dean's Park	Pr	4'0" p
3	3	Chapter House Street	CL	9'0"
4	4	Bedern Passage	P,R	5'0" p
5	"	Bedern Path	P,R	7'0" p
6	"	Penny Lane	CL,G	3'0" p
7	5	St. Andrewgate	M	7'0" p
8	6	Newgate	M	8'0"
9	"	Patrick Pool	CL	10'0"
10	7	Three Cranes Lane	CL,P,R	4'6"
11	"	Mad Alice Lane	CL,P,Y,R	3'6"
12	"	Hornpot Lane	CL,P,R	3'10"
13	8	Tonge's Court	Ch	6'0"
15	"	Queen's Path	Pw	5'7" p
16	10	Minster Gates	M	3'9" p
17	"	Stonegate	M	16'0"
18	11	Coffee Yard	CL,P,Y,G,R	2'11"
19	"	Finkle Street	CL	2'6" p
20	12	Silver Street	M	5'7" p
21	"	Little Shambles	M	10'0"
22	13	Great Shambles	M	12'0"
23	"	Shambles-to-Market	CL,P,R	3'1"
24	"	Market-to-Shambles	CL,P,R	2'3" p
25	"	Shambles-to-Market	CL,P,R	1'9" p
26	13	Market-to-Shambles	CL,P,R	4'7" p
27	"	St. Crux Passage	P,R	1'8" p
28	14	High Hungate	M	5'0"
29	"	Black Horse Passage	G,S	c. 3'0"
30	15	Foss Bridge Reach	Rv	2'8"
31	"	Straker's Passage	P,R	4'0"
32	16	Cheat's Lane	CL	10'0"
33	"	Lady Peckitts Yard	CL,P,R	4'8"
34	17	Le Kyrk Lane	CL,P,R	3'1"
35	"	All Saints' Passage	P	6'0"
36	18	Coppergate Square	Arc,R	9'0"
37	"	Foss-side Walk	Rv	3'0"
38	19	York Castle	Pw	4'0" p
39	20	St. George's Field	Pw	2'3" p
40	"	S. Esplanade	Rv	4'0" p
41	"	King's Staith	Rv	6'0" p
42	22	Ouse Walk	Rv	5'0"
43	"	Fish Landing	CL,P,R	5'0"
44	"	Church Lane	CL	7'0"
45	"	Pope's Head Alley	CL,P,R	2'7"
46	23	Hornpot-Lane-Nether	P,G,R	4'3"
47	24	Little Stonegate	M	5'0" p
49	"	Hornby's Passage	Arc,Y,R	3'2"
48	"	Pinder's Court	Arc,Y,R	3'2"
50	25	Simons' Yat	Y,P,R	4'6"

* Between posts where marked "p".

1' (1 foot) = 0,3 metre. 1" (1 inch) = 2,5 cm.

INDEX

G

H

J

K

L

M

N

O

P

Q

For your own notes....

For your own notes....

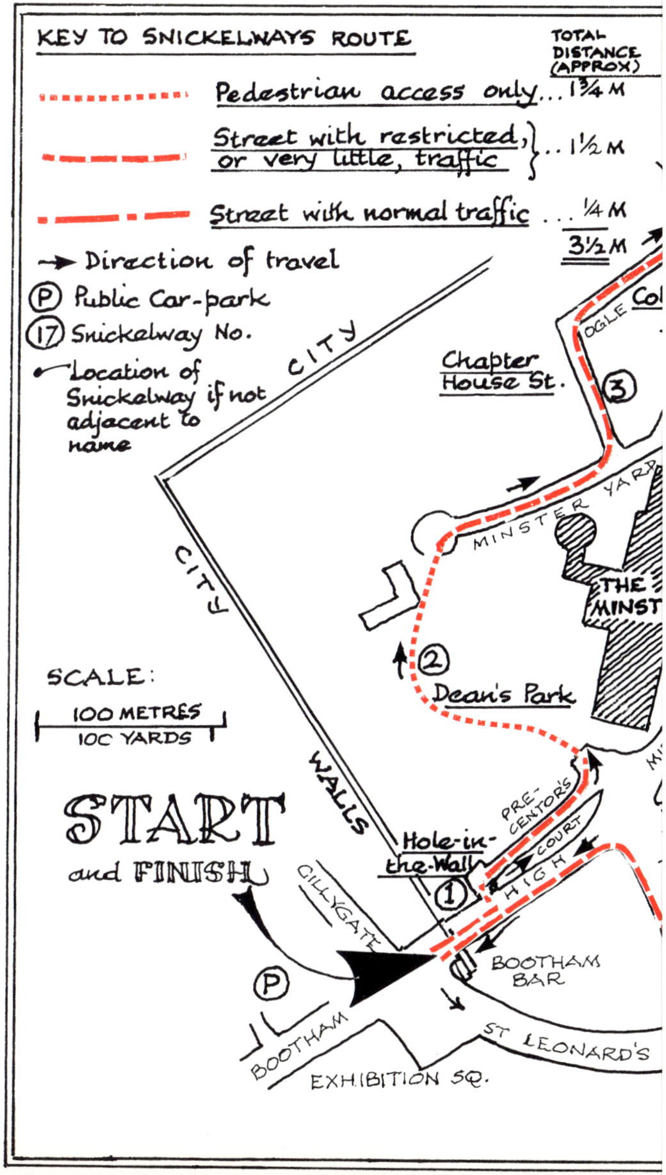
KEY TO SNICKELWAYS ROUTE
TOTAL DISTANCE (APPROX)
Pedestrian access only... 1¾ M
Street with restricted, or very little, traffic .. 1½ M
Street with normal traffic ... ¼ M
3½ M
Direction of travel
P Public Car-park
17 Snickelway No.
Location of Snickelway if not adjacent to name
SCALE:
100 METRES
100 YARDS
START and FINISH
CITY
CITY
WALLS
Chapter House St.
OGLE
MINSTER YARD
THE MINST
Dean's Park
PRE-CENTOR'S COURT
HIGH
Hole-in-the-Wall
GILLYGATE
BOOTHAM BAR
BOOTHAM
EXHIBITION SQ.
ST LEONARD'S